WINE ROUTES
OF THE CAPE

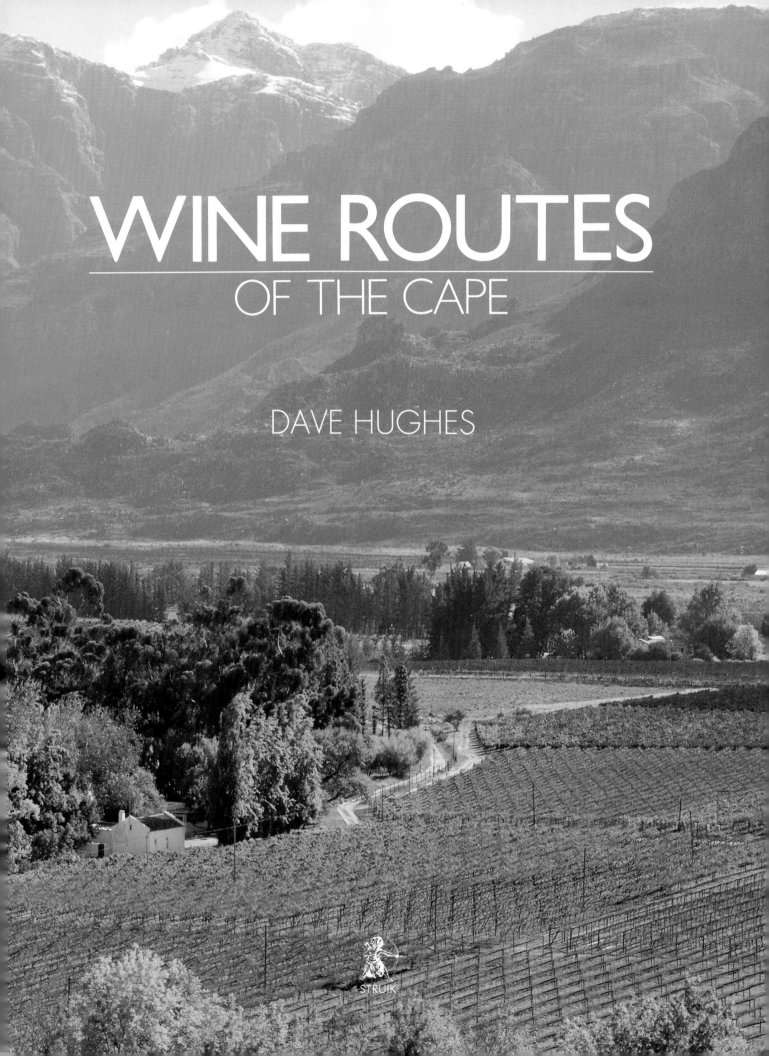

WINE ROUTES
OF THE CAPE

DAVE HUGHES

STRUIK

Struik Publishers
(a member of the Struik Group (Pty) Ltd)
80 McKenzie Street
Cape Town
8001

Reg. No.: 63/00203/07

Editor: Kevin McRae
Designer: Caroline Cluver
Cover Designer: Neville Poulter
Cartographer: Angus Carr

DTP setting by Struik DTP, Suzanne Fortescue
Reproduction by Unifoto (Pty) Ltd, Cape Town
Printed and bound by Kyodo Printing Co (Pte) Ltd, Singapore

ISBN 1 86825 182 9

Contents

Introduction 6	50 Franschhoek
Visiting the winelands 7	56 Worcester
Tasting 8	62 Robertson
Reading South African wine 9	68 Swartland
Storage 10	70 Olifants River
Cultivars 10	72 Klein Karoo
Serving wine 11	
Wine and food 12	Other regions
Food and wine checklist 13	76 *Tulbagh*
How to use this book 13	77 *Overberg*
Constantia 14	78 *Wellington*
Stellenbosch 20	79 *Durbanville*
Paarl 42	80 Index

Introduction

The history of wine making in South Africa goes right back to the days of Jan van Riebeeck. The commander of the Dutch settlement wrote to his superiors in the Netherlands asking for vine cuttings to start a vineyard soon after he arrived at the Cape, and in due course they were supplied. The first plantings took place in 1655, and, in spite of the fact that the soil was less than ideal, and that nobody at the Cape had the least idea how to run a vineyard, the plants survived: on 2 February 1659 Van Riebeeck recorded in his diary, 'Today, praise be to God, wine was pressed for the first time from Cape grapes…'. No mention is made of the quality of this product, probably because it was virtually undrinkable.

Van Riebeeck was not alone in attempting to produce wine at the Cape: in February 1657, a number of company servants were granted land in order that they might begin farming, thereby increasing the agricultural output of the settlement. Some of these newly created Free Burghers planted a few vines on their farms, and the continuation of wine making at the Cape was left in their hands after the commander left to take up a post in the East Indies.

Although the quantity of wine produced increased a little, the quality remained much the same, and the first modest exports of Cape wines met with a violently negative response. In 1679, however, Simon van der Stel was appointed as commander of the colony at the Cape. In November of that same year Van der Stel founded the town of Stellenbosch, the centre for a new community, separate from Cape Town, in which wine had a significant part to play right from the start. In 1685 he illegally procured 750 hectares of land in the Constantia valley (this he later increased to 8 500 hectares), and built a magnificent homestead on it. From the vines of his estate the commander produced the first Cape wines to meet with approval in Europe, proving that it was possible to produce quality wine at the southwestern corner of Africa.

The wine industry received a further boost in 1688 with the arrival of the French Huguenots. In an effort to escape persecution from the Catholics, these Protestants had fled France, and emigrated to the Cape with the assistance of the Dutch East India Company. Some of them had a good knowledge of viticulture, and their expertise in the subject was a valuable addition to the limited abilities of the Free Burghers.

Simon van der Stel died in 1712, and the huge estate of Constantia was divided up, the section containing the homestead being called Groot Constantia. In 1778, Hendrik Cloete bought the farm and set about making wines which attained enormous popularity not only at the Cape, but also in Europe. With the Cloetes at the helm, the Cape wine industry continued to grow steadily, until, towards the end of the 19th century, tragedy struck.

In the early 1860s, specimens of some wild grape vines were transported from America to France. In the soil around the roots of these specimens lived a species of aphid, *Phylloxera vastatrix*, which lived off the roots and leaves of the vines. The American plants had developed an immunity to the parasite, but the more sensitive, cultivated, European vines had no chance – the disease swept through the continent, wiping out 75 per cent of the vineyards and resisting all attempts at control. In 1885, *Phylloxera* reached the Cape, and it took only a few years to destroy most of the Cape's winelands. Many farmers went bankrupt and the wine industry was brought to its knees.

At first, attempts were made to combat the disease directly, but, as was the case in Europe, these were not successful, and it was finally realized that a fresh start would have to be made. The vineyards were cleared, and reconstructed by grafting vines onto *Phylloxera*-resistant American rootstocks – a practice still followed in the Cape winelands today.

The success of this scheme eventually caused further problems for the Cape wine industry, as by 1918 there was a serious overproduction of wine, which caused prices to drop substantially and resulted in the disposal of millions of unsaleable litres.

To combat this problem a controlling body was formed, the Ko-operatiewe Wijnbouwers Vereniging van Zuid-Afrika, Beperkt – more commonly known simply as the KWV. The KWV controls

January to April is the time when harvesting takes place. Although modern technology is very much a part of the wine-making process, picking is still done by hand.

South Africa's wine industry to this day, granting production quotas to producers and fixing the minimum prices to be paid for wines each year.

Grapes are now grown in all four provinces of South Africa, although grapes for quality-wine making are still confined to a very small area of the southwestern Cape, the limits of which are about 200 kilometres from Cape Town. The Cape's vineyards are among the most spectacular in the world, being set against a backdrop of towering mountains, yet still within striking distance of the sea.

This proximity to the sea is one of the factors which make the winelands one of the most popular tourist attractions in the country. Visitors can holiday by the sea, and make excursions inland to visit the vineyards and cellars.

VISITING THE WINELANDS

The wineries of the Cape range in size from large organizations, well-geared to handling visitors, to small concerns run by a family or one person. All of them, however, have one thing in common; they offer a warm and friendly welcome and are run by people who will happily explain their life's work. Nevertheless, you should not forget that wine making is their business. While they will normally welcome the opportunity of showing you around, they have much

work to do, so please be patient. It is always best to phone before setting out for a visit to make sure that the wine maker is available, if that is who you would like to see. Also be understanding: no matter how well a wine maker manages his operation or plans his day, if something goes wrong in the winery, no matter how firm your appointment, he will have to leave you and attend to the crisis.

The vineyard year is very variable, from the cold bleak winters through to the few blazing-hot days in mid-February. The height of activity in the winelands is during the vintage or harvest period which begins on the west coast in early January and continues through to early April at the cooler areas on the east coast. Because of this, the wineries and associated activities have very definite seasons when everything is happening, and others when very little is happening.

As a general rule, most wineries are open during regular business hours – with a break for lunch – in summer, while many have reduced hours during the winter months. Most wineries hire extra staff during the vintage to cope with the harvest and the extra visitors. More and more cellars are opening on Saturday afternoons, especially in the Stellenbosch and Paarl areas. Groot Constantia is the only off-sales in the country allowed to sell wine on Sundays, though hopefully this special government favour will extend to other cellars in our new, enlightened South Africa. In countries like Australia, and in California in the USA, some wineries achieve 80

Shelves of bottles line the walls at the Boschendal VIP wine-tasting room

TASTING

When visiting the wine routes you will be offered wine to taste, so that you can decide which wines you like and, consequently, which wines you will buy. The tasting of wine is a purely subjective matter, either you like what you put in your mouth or you don't, but to get the best out of the samples offered to you, there are a few basic procedures you should follow.

First lift the glass and look at the wine; you will be able to see whether the wine is red, white, or even colourless. There is a lot more you can learn from the colour of a wine, but that is for more serious tasters (if you do wish to take a more serious approach, you can consult the *Complete Book of South African Wine* by Dave Hughes, Phyllis Hands and John Kench).

Once the colour is determined, give the glass a swirl to release the smell – usually referred to as the nose. This should be attractive and lead you to actually put some of the wine in your mouth. Only a little is needed, and this should be moved around in your mouth so that it covers your tongue – then swallow slowly. It is not necessary to swallow everything that you taste; spitting is quite permissible and spittoons are supplied in wine-tasting rooms for this reason. It is practical to ensure that you have a spittoon close to you before you begin tasting.

When tasting a variety of wines, begin with dry white, then move through off-dry and semi-sweet before switching to red. Return to white late harvest before sampling sweet fortified wines at the end of the session.

Finally, do not forget that, if you are on a wine route, you will be driving from cellar to cellar to taste their products and, although you may only sample small quantities, wines contain alcohol, and alcohol and driving do not go together. One person in your party should therefore be designated as the non-drinking driver. Even if you spit everything that you taste, be very careful that the ethers do not affect you.

per cent of their total sales through Sunday visitors – Sunday is, after all, the one day in the week when many folk have the opportunity to visit the winelands.

Buying wines from the cellars you visit is certainly a very good reason for touring the winelands. However, do not forget that, if you have limited time or want to look at a range of wines from different cellars, there are some excellent wine shops scattered around the winelands: Best Cellars at Doornbosch and Oom Samie's Fine Wine Library in Dorp Street – both in Stellenbosch – La Cotte Inn Off Sales in Franschhoek, and the Weis Brothers in Main Street, Bonnievale, are leaders in their field.

Most vineyard areas have centralized information offices, where maps and brochures are available, telling you not only about the local wineries, but also restaurants, accommodation and places of interest. The wineries themselves have their own brochures and price lists, and a collection of all these can provide useful reference material when you have returned home.

You should also check the local press for information on wine events that might be taking place, such as the grape-picking and wine-making days offered by certain cellars, vintage festivals held in some of the wine regions, regional young wine shows, regional bottled-wine and food festivals, the SA Championship Show at Goodwood and the Paarl Nouveau festival on Paarl Mountain to mention a few.

An old wine press dominates the front of the Stellenryck wine museum.

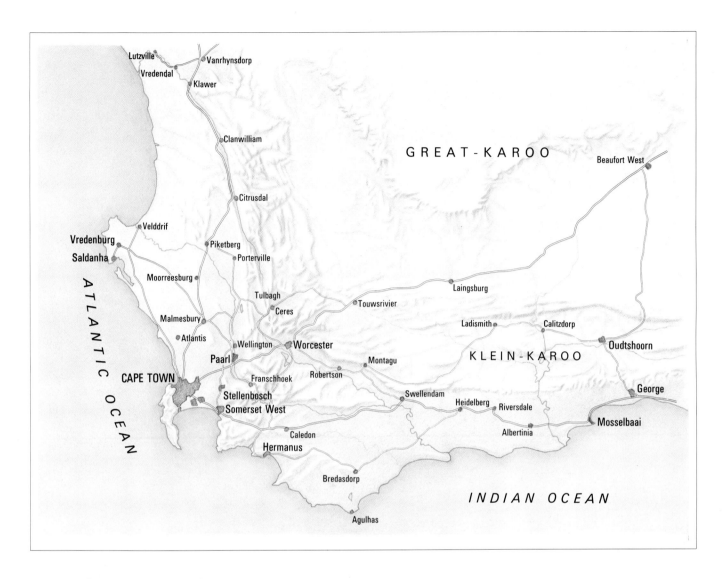

The Wine of Origin Seal adorns the necks of most South African wine bottles.

READING SOUTH AFRICAN WINE

On 1 September 1973, legislation came into force providing for one of the most comprehensive wine-control systems in the world. This laid down a set of standards to be met regarding information on the bottle outlining the origin of the wine. This system is in the process of being altered to suit the changing times, but the 'Wine of Origin Seal' will still be found on the capsule of many bottles of wine, and effectively acts as a guarantee that claims made on the label relating to the origin, vintage and cultivar of the wine are certifiably true.

ORIGIN (BLUE BAND) means that 100 per cent of the wine derives from the indicated region, district or ward (South Africa's winelands are divided by legislation into regions, which are in turn divided into districts and again into wards).

VINTAGE (RED BAND) certifies that at least 75 per cent of the wine is made from grapes harvested in the indicated year.

CULTIVAR (GREEN BAND) guarantees that the wine contains 75 per cent of the cultivar claimed, and is characteristic of that cultivar in appearance, smell and taste.

ESTATE certifies that the wine is made on the estate claimed, from grapes grown there. It need not, however, be bottled on the estate.

It is important to note that the Wine of Origin Seal is no indication of quality – until 1990 certain wines were granted 'Superior' certification, and from 1982 these bore a gold Wine of Origin Seal, but this has been discontinued.

STORAGE

If you make a purchase from a cellar, ensure that the wine is packed in a manner that will ensure that it travels safely. Most wineries are well geared to this, and will do a very professional job. However, on occasions you might buy oddly shaped bottles that could cause problems in transport, unless carefully packed.

Once home, you will need to store your wine safely. If you plan to keep your wine for any length of time, particularly if you want the flavours to develop, then it is important to store it correctly. It isn't necessary to have a large underground cellar in which to store your wines, a simple rack or shelf will do, preferably in a dark place with a reasonably constant temperature. Ideally this temperature should be between 10 and 12°C – you will not be able to maintain this through the South African summer without air conditioning, but don't panic, a temperature rise to 20°C will not adversely affect your wine. If you live next to an airport, or a busy street, try to make sure your wines are kept as stable as possible, as excess movement or vibration can damage them.

It is best to lie your bottles on their sides, with the labels facing upwards for easy reference, as this will ensure that any sediment will form along the side of the bottle, easing decanting, and that the cork is kept moist and swollen. If the cork is allowed to dry, it will shrink, letting air into the bottle and causing the wine to be damaged by oxidization.

Guard against keeping your wines for too long. Today, many wines are made ready for drinking sooner, taste them from time to time to see when they reach their peak, and enjoy them when they are at their best. If the wine is allowed to age past its best it will become uninteresting, and eventually turn to vinegar.

Traditionally, South African red wines are full-bodied, needing 10 to 20 years of maturation. Today, however, there are an increasing number of light-bodied, and some distinctly fruity, red wines available on the market. These need far less maturation, and some (the Nouveau wines, for example) are ready for immediate consumption. Judging the optimum time for an individual wine comes only with experience; it is impossible to set hard and fast rules for the maturation time of wine, as this depends on the components of the individual wines. There are, however, some rules of thumb that you can follow for ageing red wine:

CABERNETS require about 10 years, or longer, to reach their peak. (This doesn't apply to Cabernet Rosés or Cabernet Blanc de Noirs).
PINOTAGES may vary from three to nine years. For a typically young Pinotage taste with a flowery flavour, keep the wine for three years, but if you prefer a more full-bodied wine with mature character, store it for six years or more.

CULTIVARS

Many different cultivars of grapes go into the making of South Africa's various wines, sometimes individually, sometimes as part of a blend. It is not necessary to know the cultivars used to make a wine in order to enjoy it, but, for those who wish to sound knowledgeable during conversations on wine, here is a list of some of South Africa's better-known grape varieties.

WHITE CULTIVARS

BUKETTRAUBE Introduced to South Africa in the 1970s, this vigorous grower produces wines with a slightly Muscat flavour.

CAPE RIESLING (SOUTH AFRICAN RIESLING) This grape made Riesling synonymous with top-quality wines in South Africa.

CHARDONNAY This is the grape of the famous white wines of Burgundy, Chablis and Champagne in France, and it is now responsible for some of the finest wines in California. Chardonnay has become an extremely fashionable wine grape in this country.

CHENEL This cross of Chenin Blanc and Trebbiano produced by Professor Chris Orffer of the University of Stellenbosch has prospered under widely varying conditions in South Africa.

CHENIN BLANC (STEEN) This is the most widely planted of all our wine cultivars, making up more than 30 per cent of the total national crop. Good quality Steen makes both fine, fruity, dry wines and wines of any degree of sweetness, right through to the fullest botrytis wines. It makes our best sherries and is used in most of our fine sparkling wines. It is also used for sweet fortified wines and brandy production. Many wines made from this grape are not labelled with the cultivar, but carry brand names, or generic names like Blanc de Blanc.

CLAIRETTE BLANCHE This is a late-maturing grape giving low acid wine which is much appreciated in the making of sparkling wines in this country.

COLOMBAR (COLOMBARD) Originally grown for brandy production, this cultivar has, in recent years, been used to produce very attractive, fruity wines especially in the Breede River Valley Region.

FERNÃO PIREZ This Portuguese cultivar was introduced to South Africa in the 1970s, and some good wines are now being made from it.

GEWÜRZTRAMINER This important variety from Alsace in Europe does not always develop the true 'gewürz' (spicy) flavour in our growing conditions.

KERNER Introduced at the same time as Bukettraube, this grape gives a distinctive, if somewhat stern, wine.

MUSCAT D'ALEXANDRIE (HANEPOOT) This is one of the world's oldest cultivated grape varieties, and is South Africa's favourite wine grape. Hanepoot is planted in a higher percentage of South African vineyards than in any other country in the world. The wines produced from this grape have an unmistakable Muscat character.

SAUVIGNON BLANC A remarkable variety which, when used with Sémillon and Muscadel in Bordeaux, France, produces some of the most exceptional wines, including the driest Graves and the sweetest Sauternes. It is also famous on the upper Loire for the striking wines of Sancerre. In the Cape it produces outstanding wines of both the wood-aged and non-wood-aged kind.

SÉMILLON (GREEN GRAPE) This was a popular grape in the early days of South African wine making, and is the variety used in France for dry Graves and sweet Sauternes wines. It has recently started to regain a little of its original popularity in the Cape winelands.

WEISSER RIESLING (RHINE RIESLING) This variety is a relative newcomer to South Africa, and produces more fragrant wine than our traditional Cape Riesling, which, incidently, is a totally unrelated variety.

WHITE FRENCH (PALOMINO) Known locally as White French or Fransdruif, this is the same cultivar used in Spain for the production of sherry: there it is known as Palomino.

RED CULTIVARS

CABERNET FRANC Belonging to the same family as Cabernet Sauvignon, its wines are occasionally not easily identified from those of its relation; they are generally softer, however, and so make ideal blending partners. Cabernet Franc makes up only a small fraction of the national crop.

CABERNET SAUVIGNON 'King' Cabernet produces a great deal of the best Bordeaux wines, and has been transplanted to the New World probably more successfully than any other noble variety. In Bordeaux its greatest successes are in blends in varying proportions with Cabernet Franc, Malbec, Merlot and Verdot grapes. Cabernet Sauvignon makes very distinctive wines of remarkable range in style and individuality.

CINSAUT Formerly known as Hermitage, and although losing popularity, this is still by far the most widely planted red grape in South Africa. Today it is not one of the fashionable varieties, but most of South Africa's red wine is nevertheless made from it (though this is mostly bulk-produced, lower-price-range wine).

GAMAY NOIR Second in importance only to Pinot Noir in Burgundy, this is the great grape of Beaujolais. Producing excellent, full-flavoured wine ready for early drinking in the Nouveau style, it can also produce very acceptable wines for ageing.

MERLOT There is not much Merlot yet in the Cape, but encouraging quantities are being planted. Its ability to age more quickly makes it a great asset in softening the harder wines made from Cabernet Sauvignon, hence its importance in Bordeaux-style blends. It produces soft, full, attractive wines.

PINOTAGE South Africa's first commercially successful crossing, this variety was produced by Professor A. I. Perold in 1925 from Pinot Noir and Hermitage, as Cinsaut was then known. It makes wines which have a very distinct 'Pinotage ester' nose when young, but which age into good, soft reds.

PINOT NOIR This is the great cultivar of Burgundy and Champagne, but unfortunately it has not transplanted well in the New World, and is grown locally only in small amounts in the coastal region.

SHIRAZ One of the major grapes of the Rhône Valley in Europe, this variety is believed to have originated in Persia. It makes beautifully flavoured wines with a rather peculiar nose, described as 'smoky'.

Cultivar signs explain the types of grapes grown in the Delheim vineyards.

SHIRAZ wines are often soft and drinkable after three years, but, with a further three years, can mature to a very full-bodied roundness and softness.

TINTA BAROCCA does not usually require long bottle maturation, so store it for three years and then try it. Some cellars produce Tinta that develops for five to 10 years.

CINSAUT reaches its peak at three years, but, depending on how it was made, can also be left to mature for up to 10. Most Cinsauts are produced for early drinking.

White wines do not need much bottle maturation; in fact, most of them should be drunk immediately, or at least within two years from vintage. Very few local dry white wines will benefit from ageing, though there are exceptions here, such as a few dry Rieslings, some wood-aged whites, and, of course, Sauvignon Blancs and Chardonnays. A number of semi-sweet wines can benefit from storing for two to three years after vintage, and the ageing of fortified wines such as Muscadels and Jerepigos will result in a smoother character. Noble Late Harvests age with distinction over remarkably long periods.

SERVING WINE

Much has been said about the protocol of serving wine, but, essentially, if you are able to transfer the wine from bottle to glass without spilling it over anyone or anything, you have achieved all that really needs to be achieved. As regards the type of glass, tradition dictates that certain types of glasses be used for certain wines, but it is not necessary to stick rigidly to this.

For those who are interested, though, Champagne or sparkling wine is usually best served in a tall fluted glass (the wide saucer-like variety merely allows the bubbles to escape more quickly), red wine is served in a slightly larger glass than white, and fortified wines have a high alcohol content and are therefore served in very small glasses. A good wine glass should have a stem to hold it by (so that you don't heat the drink with you sweaty little hand), and a bowl large enough to hold a reasonable quantity of wine when about two thirds full. Ideally the rim of the glass should be curved slightly inward to concentrate the aroma of the wine. Glasses should be only about two thirds filled, as this allows the aroma to collect above the wine.

The instruction to serve red wines at room temperature is deceiving, room temperature can vary wildly, depending on whether it is winter or summer, and whether you have air conditioning or central heating. The ideal temperature at which to serve red wine is approximately 16˚C, while white wine should be chilled to approximately 10˚C. When chilling white wine, it is best to put the bottle in the refrigerator some two or three hours before you plan to serve it, in order that you do not over-chill the wine, thereby causing it to lose aroma and flavour. The best way to chill a wine quickly is to put the bottle into an ice bucket filled with a mixture of ice and cold water.

Late-autumn brings a blaze of colour to the Hex River Valley. The scenic splendour of the Cape's winelands is one of the reasons for their popularity as a tourist attraction.

The question of 'breathing', that is, opening the bottle some time before consumption to allow the wine to have contact with air, is really a matter of personal taste. However, a series of tests were held in 1974, in which a variety of young and old red wines were tasted immediately after opening and again one, eight and 24 hours after opening. They also tasted the same wines after they had been decanted the same intervals before tasting. The results of these tests indicated that the older the wine, the less time needed between cork pulling and tasting. Wines that are 12 years or older are usually best freshly opened, while young red wines improve with breathing. The best results with young reds are achieved by decanting. Decanting of old wines is only necessary to remove the wine from any sediment. It should be done as close to drinking as possible, and a purpose-made, glass, stopped decanter should be used.

WINE AND FOOD

Matching wine with food has become a much talked and written about subject. This is not surprising, as I doubt if there was ever in South Africa as much interest in wine as there is now.

The good old advice about red wine with red meat and white with lighter meats and seafood cannot really be faulted, except for it being so adamant. If followed you'll rarely go wrong, but oh what a boring life you would lead! Half the enjoyment of wine comes from the adventure of experiment, and the joy of having your own combination work. Most of the accepted beliefs about classic combinations of food and drink have come about more through geographic accident than culinary design anyway. Beef and Burgundy, the delicate dry wines of Alsace with pâté de foie gras, Roquefort with chilled rich Sauternes, all are regional partnerships.

Whatever you do with your experiments with wine and food, remember that strongly flavoured food will make a subtle, elegant wine lose its flavour and seem rather watery – a glorious curried oyster will destroy a delicate Blanc de Blanc. The guidelines for tasting wine should also be applied when drinking wine with meals: work from light to heavy, young to old, dry to sweet and white to red – with the exception of full-bodied sweet whites, which would be appropriate after red wine.

Besides being an accompaniment to food, wine will often enhance the flavour of a dish if used in the cooking. Food cooked with wine can be happily eaten by people whose beliefs keep them from

FOOD AND WINE CHECKLIST

The following are suggestions for matching wine to food; they are merely guidelines however, as most dishes can be made in a variety of ways, each of which can be matched with a different wine. This list can be used as a starting point, but, as it is impossible to list every conceivable dish here, you will often simply have to be creative and work out your own combinations of wine and food.

ANTIPASTO: dry or medium white
ARTICHOKES: (Vinaigrette) light-bodied red or dry rosé; (Hollandaise) full-bodied dry white
ASPARAGUS: light dry white or rosé
AVOCADO: (Vinaigrette) fino sherry; (Ritz) dry or medium white
BEEF: medium to full-bodied red
BEEF STROGANOFF: spicy or full-bodied red
BISQUES: full-bodied dry white
BOUILLABAISSE: very dry white
BREAKFAST: sparkling wine
CASSOULET: young red
CAVIAR: sparkling wine
CHEESE: Port is good with all types of cheese; (Cheddar, Gouda, Edam) any red or semi-sweet white; (Brie, Camembert) any red; (Blaukrantz, Roquefort, Danish Blue) full-bodied red; (goat's-milk cheese) fortified dessert wine

CHEESE FONDUE: light red
CHICKEN: dry white or smooth red
CHILI CON CARNE: young red
CHINESE FOOD: dry to medium white
CONSOMMÉ: dry sherry
COQ AU VIN: robust red
CRAYFISH: dry white or sparkling wine
CURRY: (mild) fruity robust white; (strong) sweet muscadel
DESSERT: sweet dessert or sparkling wine
DUCK: full-bodied semi-sweet white or dry red
ESCARGOTS: light red or rosé
FRANKFURTERS: semi-sweet white
GAME BIRDS: good smooth red
GOULASH: robust young red
GRAPEFRUIT: medium sherry
HADDOCK: full-bodied dry white
HAM: young red or semi-sweet white

HERRINGS: dry white
KIDNEYS: medium-bodied red
LAMB: good red
LINE FISH: dry or semi-sweet white
LIVER: medium-bodied red
MELON: fortified sweet wine
MINESTRONE: medium-bodied red or rosé
MUSSELS: fruity white
NUTS: port
OXTAIL: rich strong red
OYSTERS: sparkling wine, sweet or dry
PAELLA: rosé or dry white
PASTA: light red

PÂTÉ: dry white, or late harvest
PIZZA: full-bodied red
PORK: fruity white, rosé or dry red
PRAWNS: light-bodied dry white
RABBIT: young red
SALAD: dry white
SALAMI: spicy red or dry rosé
SALMON: fruity white
SOUFFLÉ: (fish) dry white; (cheese) medium-bodied red
SOUP: dry sherry
TERRINE: dry white, or late harvest, or light red
TROUT: delicate white
VEAL: smooth red
VENISON: your best red

Food and wine make an attractive combination at the Laborie Resaurant.

drinking it, because, alcohol begins to evaporate at 79°C, and will disappear long before any simmering or boiling temperature is reached – only the delicious flavour remains. If a recipe calls for liquid, it is a good idea to replace some of that liquid with wine, but the amount of wine used should rarely exceed a third to half the liquid required. Wine should be considered a seasoning and take its place alongside your herbs on the kitchen shelf.

HOW TO USE THIS BOOK

This book is a guide to one of South Africa's most popular tourist attractions – the wine routes of the southwestern Cape. There are nine such wine routes, each of which has been given a separate chapter. Each chapter has a general introduction giving a background to the area, mentioning some other attractions, and occasionally giving suggestions on how best to tackle the route. Each chapter also has a map which shows the location of the wineries: a building with a rounded gable denotes an estate, one with a pointed gable a private cellar, and one with no gable any other kind a winery.

The wineries on the route are listed alphabetically, and each is given a write up comprising an introduction, a section of useful information (address, telephone number, sales and tasting times, other attractions etc.), and a list of wines produced, with a star rating for each wine. The star ratings have been taken from the *South African Wine Buyer's Guide*, which uses a five-star grading system. Stars in brackets indicate half a star. Some wines have not been covered in the *Wine Buyer's Guide* – or, in the case of nouveau wines, not rated – these are the one's with '(no rating)' next to their names. Wherever possible, prices (for tasting, meals, tours etc.) have been given but, as inflation renders these inaccurate fairly quickly, these should be seen simply as a guide.

There are many farms open to the public which are not on the official wine routes in the area, and these have been covered at the end of each relevant chapter, also in alphabetical order. There is also a section at the end of the book covering regions which do not have wine routes – Tulbagh, Overberg, Wellington and Durbanville – but which do have wineries open to the public.

It is up to you to plan your route using the information given in this guide; you may choose to visit wineries only on one route, or select from two or more routes (as long as the distances are not too great). Whatever you choose, you are sure to enjoy a memorable experience while exploring this beautiful southwestern corner of the Cape.

Constantia

The Constantia Wine Route is one of the Cape's newer wine routes, in spite of the fact that the wine-growing region is the oldest. As early as the 17th Century, Simon van der Stel, founder and first owner of Constantia, invited visitors to the Cape to tour his vineyards and cellars. With such a history, such idyllic surroundings, and so many attractions to offer tourists, it is no wonder that this route is luring as many visitors as it does.

The smallest of the wine routes, it is, at the moment, made up of three farms, all of which were once part of Governor Van der Stel's original Constantia Estate. It was here that Van der Stel planted grapes and did so much to improve the Cape's wine – the wines of Constantia developed an early, almost legendary reputation for their unusual quality. After the Governor's death in 1712, Constantia was divided into a number of farms, some of which have, over the years, been covered by the urban sprawl and forever lost to grape growing and wine making. Fortunately, Buitenverwachting and Klein Constantia have reversed this trend, and others are now following. Groot Constantia has remained as a farm throughout its long history and has always been involved with wines even though its production of wine has not been continuous. Bottling of its wine in the modern era dates back to 1960.

The Constantia valley is overshadowed (literally, shade comes early in the afternoon and helps the general cooling of conditions in the area), by the 600-metre-high Constantiaberg. This, together with the sea breezes coming in off False Bay, makes Constantia one of the coolest wine-growing areas in the Cape, a factor which helps with the production of stylish white wines and reds of great character.

A tour of the Constantia Wine Route would be incomplete without a visit to the Alphen Hotel as, although the Alphen estate no longer exists and Alphen wines are no longer made there, the name of Alphen is very much a part of the history of wine-making in the Cape. The property was originally granted to a Free Burgher in the late 17th century. Later, it was transferred to Simon van der Stel, who kept it separate from his Constantia estate. After Van der Stel's death, the VOC granted the property to Theunis Dirkz van Schalkwyk in 1714, refusing to recognize the claims of the Governor's heirs. In the years that followed, Alphen underwent several changes of ownership, until Abraham Lever took it over in 1748 and started building the homestead that today forms part of the hotel. In 1814, the estate was taken over by Dirk Cloete, whose descendant, Peter Bairnsfather Cloete, now owns the hotel. Urban development has taken its toll on Alphen; by the late 1960s, wine making had stopped on the estate. Peter Cloete then purchased land near Stellenbosch and continued production of the Alphen wines from there. In 1972, however, the distribution of Alphen wines was taken over by Gilbeys, and the old winery at Alphen in Constantia, was turned into a library by the Cape Divisional Council. In spite of this, the atmosphere of gracious living in bygone days still lingers at the hotel.

The hotel's restaurant (Tel. (021) 794 5011) should not be overlooked as a place to eat. Excellent food can be enjoyed in the historic atmosphere of the dining room – just be sure to book ahead. The Alphen Bottle Store is on the same premises as the hotel, and is the home of the Alphen Wine of the Month Club, the successful brainchild of Colin Collard which has prompted the start of a number of similar wine clubs.

For those who would like a diversion from things winy, the Old Cape Farm Stall (near the entrance to Groot Constantia) is worth a visit. All the favourites one can expect from a farm stall are here (loads of fresh fruit and veg, home baking and bottling), as well as some interesting additions such as home-made pasta. A restaurant (Tel. (021) 794 2034) serves teas and lunches, with champagne breakfasts being a feature on Sundays. The farm stall is open from 08h00 to 18h00 daily. The lecture centre for the Cape Wine Academy is on the same premises.

*Autumn tinges the vineyards of the Constantia Valley with gold. The cool temperatures of
the valley are a vital factor in ensuring the production of high-quality wines.*

BUITENVERWACHTING

Overseas investment, youthful staff and a total commitment to quality has brought this old farm back to life. Originally part of the Bergvliet division of Constantia, Buitenverwachting was sold as a further subdivision in 1793. It has since had many owners and wine production was stopped for a time.

This changed when the estate was purchased by Richard Muller in 1981. The area of the farm was increased, the vineyards replanted, the homestead and historic buildings restored, and an attractive, ultra-modern, thatched-roof cellar constructed.

Buitenverwachting's maiden vintage was in 1985. Wine making has been careful and conservative and has resulted in some exceptionally good wines, fitting the area's long-standing reputation for quality. Its wines are now regular winners at the International Wine and Spirit Competition in Britain.

ADDRESS: Buitenverwachting, Klein Constantia Road, Constantia 7800.
TELEPHONE: (021) 794 5190/1
FAX: (021) 794 1351
WINE SALES AND TASTING:
Weekdays: 09h00 to 17h00
Saturdays: 09h00 to 13h00
Tastings cost R1-50 a head.
CELLAR TOURS: Guided cellar tours are run on weekdays at 11h00 and 15h00 from November to February, or by appointment for the rest of the year.
RESTAURANT: The Buitenverwachting restaurant is superbly situated amongst the farm buildings with excellent views across the vineyards of the towering Constantiaberg. It is highly regarded for its fine, award-winning cuisine. Booking essential (Tel. (021) 794 3522).

WINES:
Blanc Fumé ★★★★ The 1986 vintage produced only 8 000 bottles of this beautiful wine. Big, rich and complex when launched, it has developed beautifully and has the potential to develop even more. The 1988 is made from high-sugar almost late-harvest grapes – it is a big, complex wine.
Buitenkeur ★★★★ This blend from the 1986 vintage will be the cellar's entry into the Bordeaux style of wines made in the Cape. It spent 14 months in new Nevers oak before it was bottled. A little more than half the blend is Cabernet, with the balance being Merlot plus a fraction of Cabernet Franc. It is deep in colour and character with the Cabernet showing strongly through good oak.
Sauvignon Blanc ★★★★ The 1988 shows a change in style for the better. Good cultivar nose (lots of khakibos), lots of penetrating clean flavour. It tastes very good right now, but with time it will develop further into a fine drinking wine.
Buiten Blanc ★★★(★)
Noblesse ★★★(★)
Rhine Riesling ★★★(★)
Blanc de Noir ★★★
Pinot Gris ★★(★)
L'Arrivée (no rating)

GROOT CONSTANTIA

A visit to Groot Constantia offers a very special walk through Cape history. Dating way back to Simon van der Stel it has followed the Cape's agricultural and social history right up to the very modern cellar it boasts today.

Governor Van der Stel definitely took advantage of his position to acquire all the property he consolidated to create his model estate, Constantia. His meticulous attention to detail and use of the latest scientific methods of the day – in particular the hygienic care of his wine making – led to the estate's great reputation. The 'Governor's' wine became much sought after.

After Simon van der Stel's death in 1712, the estate was divided into three main sections, and eventually subdivided further. The portion retaining the homestead and wine cellars was named Groot Constantia. In 1885, the estate was sold to the Cape Colonial government and it was run as an experimental farm until 1975. Due to the development of Constantia as a residential area its usefulness as an experimental farm declined, and in 1976 Groot Constantia was transferred to a board of control. It is now managed as though it were a private estate, and is probably South Africa's best-known wine trademark.

There is no doubt that Simon van der Stel knew what he was doing when he selected the site for his great farm. Lying in the east-facing lee of Table Mountain, it is blessed with an exceptionally cool climate and receives good regular rain and has deep rich mountain soil.

Over recent years, sections of the original Groot Constantia estate have been acquired and consolidated into what it was during the late 18th century, when it was owned by the famous wine maker, Hendrik Cloete. The estate still evokes the popular memory of its near

The magnificent Buitenverwachting homestead has been lovingly restored to its former splendour. The name means 'beyond expectation'.

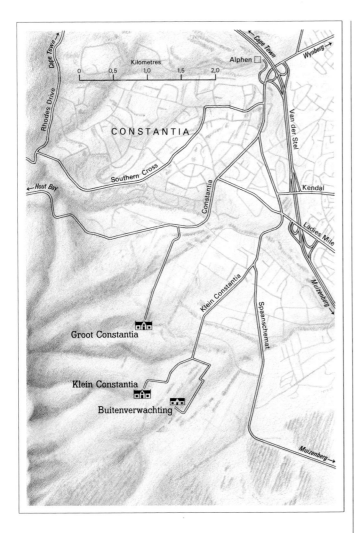

legendary wines of the 17th and 18th centuries – the rich, sweet wines so often written about, that kept the royal houses of Europe and the poets and writers of the day happy during their cold northern winters with the warm glow of Cape sunshine in their glasses or goblets; the wines which Napoleon drank to ease his last days while exiled on Elba. It is an estate blessed with a most beautiful setting and some of the finest examples of old Cape architecture to be found anywhere.

This small section of the once-vast Simon van der Stel property draws close to a quarter of a million visitors a year from every part of South Africa and all around the world. They come to explore the beautifully restored homestead and cellars, to meander along its tree-lined avenues and wonder at the beauty that was gazed upon by Hendrik Cloete and the famous diarist Lady Anne Barnard in those far off days.

The beautiful buildings designed by Louis Thibault and executed by Anton Anreith are still very much part of a revitalized modern farming concern. Cloete's magnificent cellar is now a wine museum, while the modern cellar ensures the continued production of quality wine. Each day modern farming activity carries on, undisturbed by the hundreds of tourists who arrive to take a look back into history.

Groot Constantia is a registered estate, and its wines are entirely grown, crushed, matured and bottled on the premises. One of the particular peculiarities that irks other cellar owners but pleases Groot Constantia and its visitors is that it can sell its wine on Sundays.

ADDRESS: Groot Constantia State Estate, Private Bag, Constantia 7848.
TELEPHONE: (021) 794 5128
WINE SALES AND TASTING: Daily 10h00 to 17h00
(Open every day of the year except Christmas Day and Good Friday) Tastings take place during sales hours. The cost is R3-50, which includes the price of a glass and allows the tasting of five wines.
CELLAR TOURS: Excellent guided cellar tours including an audio-visual display and wine tasting are conducted seven days a week, hourly between 10h00 and 17h00. The cost is R3-50 a head. The tours are usually held in English and Afrikaans, but German-, French- and Dutch-language tours can be organized by appointment.
RESTAURANTS: The Jonkershuis Restaurant specializes in traditional Cape lunches and teas. It is open seven days a week from 10h00 to 17h00, and, depending on the weather, one can either sit inside, or out under the oaks. For reservations phone (021) 794 6255. The Tavern serves either a warm or cold buffet and features wine by the glass, schnitzel and strudel. They often cater for functions, so it may be a good idea to book beforehand. It is open daily from 10h00 to 17h00, but is closed on Mondays. For reservations phone (021) 74 1144
HISTORICAL ATTRACTIONS: The homestead is a museum featuring furniture of the Dutch East India Company era. An admission fee of R2-00 is charged except to pensioners, children and students, who are allowed in free.
The Groot Constantia Wine Museum is situated in the historic cellars. Also look out for Van der Stel's famous bath.
WALKS: There are walks on the estate to various lookout points from where Van der Stel's bath and the entire Constantia valley can be viewed.
WINES:

Cabernet Sauvignon ★★★★ The Cabernets of Groot Constantia have an enviable reputation of elegance and refinement. Some years ago the wine varied quite considerably from bottle to bottle, but today quality is consistent. Always an interesting Cabernet, it makes a good medium-bodied wine after ageing. Recent vintages probably need only five to six years to reach their best and the ageing in good, new small wood has added some much-needed complexity.
Gewürtztraminer ★★★★ A very good off-dry version of the cultivar. Full Gewürtztraminer nose with plenty of flavour.
Gouveneurs Reserve ★★★★ The first vintage launched was the 1986. A medium-bodied, wood-aged wine blended from Cabernet Sauvignon and Cabernet Franc. To my mind this is the best red yet produced from this cellar.
Shiraz ★★★★ The Shiraz is usually Constantia's best wine and consistently one of South Africa's better Shirazes – evidence that many of the country's best reds come from the cooler growing areas.
Blanc Fumé ★★★(★)
Chardonnay ★★★(★)
Heerenrood ★★★(★)
Weisser Riesling ★★★(★)
Blanc de Blanc ★★★
Constantia Blanc ★★★
Constantia Rood ★★★
Noble Late Harvest ★★★
Pinotage ★★★
Pinot Noir ★★★
Rooi Dessert ★★★
Sauvignon Blanc ★★★
Vintage Port ★★★
Bouquet Blanc ★★(★)
Special Late Harvest ★★(★)
Constantia Rosé ★★
Late Harvest ★★
Stein ★★
Pinot Gris (no rating)

The gates of Groot Constantia admit thousands of tourists to the estate every year.

The Groot Constantia manor house was originally a double-storey building. It was Hendrik Cloete who turned the ground floor into cellars and raised the ground in front up to the top floor.

KLEIN CONSTANTIA

When Dougie Jooste bought Klein Constantia in June 1980, it was his avowed intent to bring the legendary name of Constantia back into the forefront of the world of wine. To do this he needed the best vineyards possible, and today these can be seen on the slopes of the Constantiaberg – some of the very best you will see anywhere in the world.

When Dougie first saw Klein Constantia the farm was in a somewhat dilapidated state (the land was almost completely overgrown with bush and Port Jackson trees, and numerous wrecks of lorries and old cars were dotted about), but he had no hesitation in buying as he had been searching for a farm for 10 years.

The estate's fine wines have developed a remarkable reputation for being the Cape's best in an amazingly short period of time. One of Dougie Jooste's dreams was to bring back 'the sweet, luscious and excellent wine of Constantia' that was drunk by Frederick the Great, the King of England, the King of France, Napoleon and anyone who was anybody, but which disappeared from the scene some 100 years ago. In July 1982, selected grapes, including a special clone of Muscat de Frontignan, were planted on the lower slopes in Klein Constantia's vineyards. In 1986, the talented young wine maker, Ross Gower, made the first modern *Vin de Constance*. This wine was aged for four years before eventually being launch at the end of 1990. The legend had been reborn.

Vin de Constance epitomizes the commitment to fine wine by all involved at Klein Constantia. The wines they make are magnificent,

the vineyards the best and their cellars superlative. In fact, the underground, vaulted cellars designed by Gawie Fagan, received the Award of Merit from the Institute of South African Architects, making this the only South African winery to have achieved such a distinction.

Klein Constantia's maiden wine, an '86 Sauvignon Blanc, was judged the South African Champion White wine in that year. Since then, their Cabernets have, for two years in a row, been the best on show. However, the real proof of just how good the estate's wines are is in your tasting.

ADDRESS: Klein Constantia Estate, P. O. Box 375, Constantia 7848
TELEPHONE: (021) 794 5188
WINE SALES AND TASTING:
Weekdays: 09h00 to 13h00 and 14h00 to 17h00
Saturdays: 09h00 to 13h00
Tastings are free of charge.
CELLAR TOURS: Guided tours are conducted by appointment.
WINES:

Cabernet Sauvignon ★★★★★
The 1988 vintage was released in mid-1990. This very impressive wine has super cultivar flavours and is well wooded.

Chardonnay ★★★★★ I tasted it first with the Australian Chardonnay master, Len Evans, and he fully agreed that the first Chardonnay wine from the 1988 vintage was one of the best in the Cape. Cellar samples of the 1989 and 1990 suggest that future releases will be well worth waiting for.
Sauvignon Blanc ★★★★★ New Zealand is currently supposed to be making the best Sauvignon Blancs in the world, and Ross Gower, the wine maker at Klein Constantia, spent a few years working there after leaving Nederburg, where he

had his initial training under Gunter Brözel. No doubt the experience he gained, together with the magnificent fruit from this estate, has enabled this talented young man to produce such a tremendous Sauvignon Blanc. Like so many South African wines of great character, it has a high alcohol content of almost 13 per cent, and is undoubtedly one of the Cape's great wines. The wine which won the white wine championship at the 1986 Young Wine Show was also a Sauvignon Blanc from this same cellar but it is being kept for later release. Neither wine has had any wood-ageing, as the wine maker believes that wood would detract from his wine rather than enhance it. The 1988 is an even bigger wine than the 1986. It will develop well over four to five years.

Blanc de Blanc ★★★★ A big, beautiful wine at 13 per cent alcohol, produced because the estate believed its Sauvignon Blanc from the 1987 vintage was not up to their style and standard. It was blended with Chenin Blanc to produce South Africa's best combination of these two varieties. As good as it tasted when released, it should develop well over four to five (maybe more) years.

Rhine Riesling ★★★★ The 1986 is the first vintage released from this estate. It is not quite semi-sweet, but igives an initial impression of dryness. It is a delightfully well-flavoured wine which is soft on the palate and very easy to drink. It is developing with considerable benefit and should continue to do so over another year or two. The 1988 vintage continues the same high-class style.

Noble Late Harvest (no rating)

Klein Contstantia was separated from the original Constantia estate in 1819. The estate experienced a succession of owners and mixed fortunes until Dougie Jooste took it over.

Stellenbosch

The name of Stellenbosch is famous throughout the world of wine. At about the time Dom Perignon was putting the bubbles into champagne (1688-1715) Simon van der Stel gave his name to a campsite that has now developed into the main centre for quality wine production in the Cape. After the establishment of the town in 1679, Stellenbosch developed rapidly. In 1682, it received its first local authority, and it became the seat of a magistrate in 1685. Right from the start, vines were grown for wine production, and the very earliest mentions of the town and district refer to its wine.

Simon van der Stel held a particular love for the town he founded, and celebrated his birthday there each year. The occasion became the major festive event of the year, and the locals gathered for sports, feasts and shooting competitions. At one time parrots were hunted on 'Papegaaiberg'; the hunts were later replaced by target shoots using parrot-shaped targets. To this day, one of the Gilbeys trademarks shows a 'polly' with an arrow through it. Van der Stel's birthday is re-enacted annually on the Braak – the open public area in the centre of the town.

It was Van der Stel who ordered the planting of the oak trees in Stellenbosch – trees which have led to the town being nicknamed 'Eikestad' (oak town). A school was established in 1683, and in 1881 Victoria College came into being. The college grew, and in 1918 it was awarded higher status, becoming the University of Stellenbosch. Today the university's 40 000 students dominate the town socially, culturally and sports wise.

The town is recognized as South Africa's wine capital – the Stellenbosch region being made up of some 23 estates, 18 private cellars, and five co-ops – and is home to the country's three major liquor companies (Distiller's Corporation, Stellenbosch Farmers' Winery and Gilbeys) and the international headquarters of the Rembrandt Group founded by Dr Anton Rupert.

Every effort is made to preserve the character and atmosphere of Stellenbosch, and the wine, brandy and tobacco industries have contributed greatly in this respect. The Stellenbosch Village Museum covers two blocks in the oldest part of town, and features houses from different periods of over two centuries of history. The Schroederhuis of 1790 is the oldest restored house in the country; Blettermanhuis is an example of a wealthy home of the mid-18th century; Grosvenor House reflects the gracious Batavian period and the second British occupation; and Olaf Bergh house shows the styles of the Victorian period. The museum is open on weekdays and Saturdays from 09h30 to 17h00, and on Sundays and religious holidays from 14h00 to 17h00.

The importance of both wine and brandy in the history of Stellenbosch can be seen at the Stellenryck Wijn Museum and the Oudemeester Brandy Museum. The building that now contains the Stellenryck museum was erected in 1780 and is situated at the corner of Dorp Street and the Strand road. It houses a collection of artifacts tracing the history of wine. The Oudemeester museum on Aan den Wagenweg – off Dorp Street – comprises a number of Sir Herbert Baker cottages housing over 1 000 items illustrating the history of brandy. Both museums are open on weekdays from 09h00 to 17h00 and on Saturdays from 10h00 to 17h00.

Around the Stellenbosch region, there is plenty to offer the visitor hours of enjoyment and pleasure. Apart from the farms and co-ops of the Stellenbosch Wine Route, tourists can visit the cellars of the major merchants, a host of other cellars and a wide choice of eateries. For those who enjoy Italian cuisine, both De Cameron in Plein Street (Tel. (02231) 3331) and Mama Roma in the Stelmark Centre (Tel. (02231) 6064) are excellent choices (the latter is one of the 10 most popular restaurants in the Cape, and the former has excellent seasonal eating such as perlemoen and wild mushrooms)

– and both have good wine lists. Ralph's, tucked away in a little alley off Andringa Street (Tel. (02231) 3532), is known for its good food and generous portions. Take your own wine though, as the restaurant is unlicensed.

On the Strand road, at the rear of the Doornbosch complex, is the thatched, cottage-style building that houses the Doornbosch restaurant (Tel. (02231) 7 5079). Continental and popular Cape Dutch dishes are served here, and the restaurant is open for both lunch and dinner, though not on Sundays. Also at the Doornbosch complex is the Doornbosch wine house, a specialist wine shop which has a wonderful collection of older vintages – if they have not got what you want, they will try to locate it for you.

Another specialist wine shop is Oom Samie's Fine Wine Library at 84 Dorp Street, which specializes in the best wines of the area and older vintages. Arrangements will be made to ship your purchase to any part of the world. The wine library is on the premises of Oom Samie se Winkel, a throwback to the general dealer of long ago. The visitor to this shop will be greeted by a potpourri of evocative smells, and traditional wares strung and shelved from floor to ceiling. Old-fashioned sweets, rolls of chewing tobacco, bokkoms, calabashes, wicker baskets, leather whips, sharkskin – you name it, Oom Samie se Winkel has got it.

If you feel like a bit of a change from wine, you could visit the Van Rhyn's Brandy Cellar and Cooperage (Van Rhyn Road, Vlottenburg Station, Stellenbosch District, Tel. (02231) 9 3875). Guided tours of the cellar and cooperage are run at specific times (weekdays: 09h30, 10h30, 11h30, 14h30, and 15h30), and these finish with a tasting of various brandies.

For those who wish to stay in the Stellenbosch area, rather than drive in from Cape Town, a wide choice of types and styles of accommodation is offered, ranging from the five-star Lord Charles near Somerset West to the bed and breakfast establishments either in the vineyards or situated in central Stellenbosch. Contact your local tourist information centre for specific details.

Rose bushes add splashes of colour to the vineyards at the Oude Libertas amphitheatre – a cultural centre for Stellenbosch, which hosts a variety of entertainment in the summer.

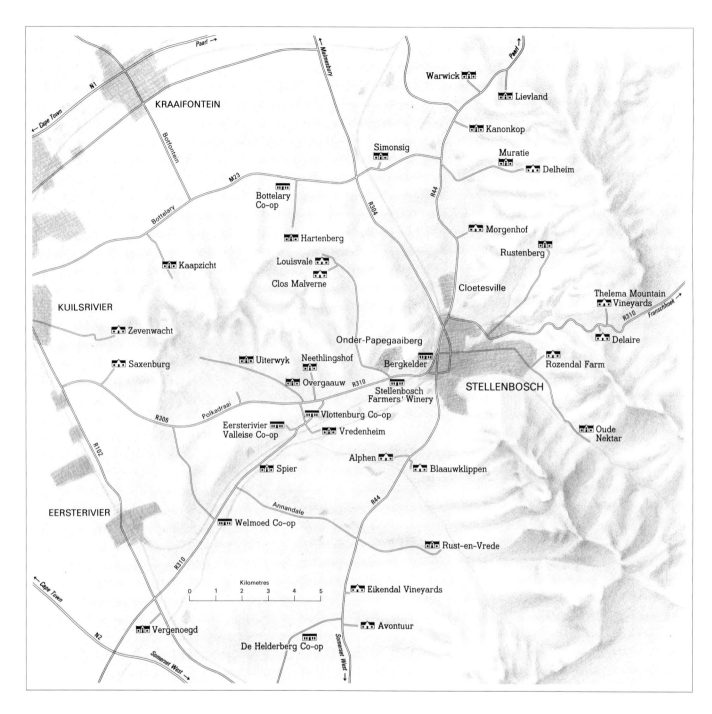

AVONTUUR

Not quite halfway between Stellenbosch and Somerset West, and at the foot of the Helderberg, Avontuur spreads its paddocks and vineyards over the lower slopes of the famous mountains. The attractive paddocks are the breeding ground of impressive race horses; in 1989, the July winner, Right Prerogative, was tragically killed in a horse transporter accident when returning to the Cape. Alongside the paddocks are the vineyards that supply the newly built, slightly Victorian-styled cellar with the grapes to produce wines packaged with innovative, imaginative and colourful labels.

Estate manager, Manie Kloppers, and wine maker, Jean Luc Sweerts initially made a name with their 1989 Chardonnay, but unfortunately the 1990 vintage is not up to the same standard. However, the overall range from this winery is of good quality and the farm is well geared to receive visitors. The luncheon area has the most magnificent view across False Bay and over the Cape Flats to the rear of Table Mountain in the distance.

ADDRESS: Avontuur, P. O. Box 1128, Somerset West 7130
TELEPHONE: (024) 55 3450
FAX: (024) 55 4600
WINE SALES AND TASTING:
Weekdays: 08h30 to 17h00
Saturdays: 08h30 to 12h00
Tastings cost 30c each.
CELLAR TOURS: Guided cellar tours are run by appointment.
SHOP: A few souvenirs may be bought in the wine-tasting room.
TOURS: A tour of the stables is available by appointment.
WINES:

Le Chardon ★★★★ One of the biggest surprises from the 1989 vintage was the first release of this cultivar from this cellar. It has good cultivar nose and attractive toffee, toasty taste. This wine drank very well on release, but the quantities are limited, so very little will be kept to see its development in the bottle.
Cabernet Sauvignon ★★★(★)
Grand Vin Blanc ★★★(★)
Blanc de Noir ★★★
Pinotage ★★★
Nuit St Pierre Vin Blanc ★★(★)
Vin Blanc ★★(★)
Blanc de Blanc ★★
Chardonnay (no rating)

BLAAUWKLIPPEN

Blaauwklippen, one of the more established of the modern wineries, is situated on the foothills of the Helderberg, close to Stellenbosch, and is easy to find with its well-marked entrance almost opposite that of the Stellenbosch Technopark. The farm is owned by Graham Boonzaaier, but it was wine maker Walter Finlayson who brought the winery on stream with the first bottlings in 1975. The cellar's many fine wines have received much acclaim, and won all kinds of awards both locally and internationally. Finlayson won the very first Diners Club award for Wine Maker of the Year with his 1980 Zinfandel, and then repeated the success the next year with his 1980 Cabernet Sauvignon.

Walter has now left to farm his own estate and his assistant of six years, Jacques Kruger, is the man in charge. Jacques continues to uphold the cellar's reputation for producing excellent wines.

Blaauwklippen has for years run a most successful Blending Competition, where amateur enthusiasts from all over the country can test their skills using base wines supplied by the cellar.

Visitors are welcome, and the estate is well geared – especially during the tourist season – to cater for them. They have a wonderful collection of horse-drawn carriages (some of which have given their names to Blaauwklippen wines – Red and White Landau, Barouche, etc.) and magnificent horses to pull them.

Blaauwklippen is also the home of Medallion mushrooms, although this is not open to the public.

ADDRESS: Blaauwklippen,
P. O. Box 54, Stellenbosch 7600
TELEPHONE: (02231) 90 0133/4
FAX: (02231) 90 1250
WINE SALES AND TASTING: Sales Weekdays: 09h00 to 16h45
Saturdays: 09h00 to 12h45
Wine may be tasted on weekdays from 09h00 to 12h45 and from 14h00 to 16h00, and on Saturdays from 09h00 to 12h30. A booklet of five coupons (one coupon per tasting) costs R1-50 and the coupons are also valid at Delheim, Eersterivier, Vlottenburg and Welmoed; glasses must be bought, a tulip glass costing R3-50 plus tax and a tumbler costing R1-80 plus tax.
CELLAR TOURS: From 1 December to 31 January, guided cellar tours are conducted on demand. For the rest of the year, they take place at 11h00 and 15h00.
RESTAURANT: From October to the end of April, an excellent coachman's lunch is served between 12h00 and 14h00, Monday to Saturday (R14-75). For large groups, booking is essential.
SHOP: A shop sells weinwurst, jams, chutneys and general souvenirs during wine sales hours.
HISTORICAL ATTRACTIONS: A museum boasts an extensive collection of Cape furniture, kitchen utensils and coaches.
TOURS: From November to the end of March coach rides around the vineyards are offered from 10h00 to 12h00 and 14h00 to 16h00 at a cost of R1-00 for adults and 50c for children.
WINES:
Cabernet Sauvignon ★★★★(★) This is a light style of Cabernet with a decidedly Bordeaux character. Blaauwklippen Cabernet needs from six to eight years to develop to its full potential.
Noble Late Vintage ★★★★(★) A powerfully flavoured wine with superb botrytis character. It ages beautifully.
Barouche ★★★★ The first release was a blend of 90 per cent Pinot Noir and 10 per cent Chardonnay, resulting in a pink *méthode champenoise* wine with a beautiful nose and fine flavour. It was launched with the 1984 vintage and has developed well in the bottle. The 1987 has good flavour and was released in mid-1990.
Pinot Noir ★★★★ This rather fickle variety has baffled most wine makers beyond the borders of Burgundy. Walter Finlayson persevered with the cultivar, however, and was particularly successful with it. He has established himself as the pioneer and is now the expert in the Cape with this cultivar.
Port ★★★(★)
Sauvignon Blanc ★★★(★)
Shiraz ★★★(★)
Special Late Vintage ★★★(★)
Special Late Vintage Reserve ★★★(★)
Zinfandel ★★★(★)
Blanc de Noir ★★★
Cabriolet ★★★
Chardonnay ★★★
Muscat Ottonel ★★★
Red Landau ★★★
Rhine Riesling ★★★
White Landau ★★★
Nouveau (no rating)

The omnibus (of French origin) now used to ferry visitors around the vineyards at Blaauwklippen once transported commuters between Cape Town and Claremont.

BOTTELARY CO-OPERATIVE

This large co-op on the Bottelary hills produces a large range of wines to suit a wide cross-section of palates. They have produced consistently good Gewürztraminers and Noble Late Harvests, and were the first co-op ever to have a wine selected for South African Airways' international flights.

Each year, on the last Saturday in February, they hold a consumers' harvest day where you can pick and crush your own grapes and have a jolly good time while at it. The day includes a breakfast of sandwiches and sparkling wine in the vineyards, and the grape-picking is followed by a braai – with live entertainment – at lunch time. The Harvest Day wine is issued under a special label. Tickets for the harvest day are available from 1 January.

ADDRESS:Bottelary Co-op,
P. O. Box 16, Koelenhof 7605
TELEPHONE: (02231) 9 2204
FAX: (02231) 9 2205
WINE SALES AND TASTING:
Weekdays: 08h30 to 12h30 and
13h30 to 17h00
Saturdays: 08h30 to 13h00
Wines may be tasted for R2-00
(glass and tasting).
CELLAR TOURS: Guided cellar tours
can be arranged by appointment.
SHOP: Various souvenirs can be
bought at the wine-tasting room.
WINES:
Gewürztraminer ★★★★ The 1983
was Stellenbosch's Champion
White Cultivar trophy winner at the
South African Championship Wine
Show, and gold-medal winner at
the Stellenbosch Bottled Wine
Show. All these honours leave no

doubt that this is a very good wine
indeed. The fine wine from 1989
has a lovely rose-petal nose and
good flavour.
Pinotage ★★★(★)
Riesling ★★★(★)
Shiraz ★★★(★)
Weisser Riesling ★★★(★)
Adelroodt ★★★
Bukettraube ★★★
Cabernet Sauvignon ★★★
Sauvignon Blanc ★★★
Blanc de Blanc ★★(★)
Chenin Blanc ★★(★)
Vin Sec ★★(★)
Blanc de Noir ★★
Chardonnay ★★
Goue Muskaat ★★
Late Harvest ★★
Noble Late Harvest ★★
Port ★★

CLOS MALVERNE

Claimed to be the smallest winery in Stellenbosch, this cellar is hard to miss as it has one of the largest signs on the wine route. If you take the Devon Valley road from Stellenbosch you will pass a school on your left at about four kilometres; another kilometre further on is an awkward turn to the left. Take this turn, and half a kilometre along the road, on the right, is Clos Malverne.

The estate is owned by Seymour Pritchard, with wine making done by Jeremy Walker. It is tiny, but nonetheless produces excellent wines, specializing in reds. Jeremy has produced good Cabernet, great Pinotage and an excellent flagship wine called Auret. The first vintage of this wine was 1988 and it is all wood-aged Cabernet, but subsequent vintages will contain Merlot. Jeremy believes in Pinotage, so this will be another product to watch from this very new cellar, which has already been a prize winner at the young wine shows, and trophy winner in 1990 for the best South African wood-matured red.

Jeremy Walker has an interesting background; after obtaining his degree at Stellenbosch University, and working for a short time at Bertrams and then in Germany and France, he returned to South Africa to study for a Masters degree in Business Administration at the University of Cape Town. He then moved away from wine making, joining BP, and followed this up with a series of his own business ventures before returning to wine making. And what a return!

ADDRESS: Clos Malverne,
P. O. Box 187, Stellenbosch 7602
TELEPHONE: (02231) 3528
WINE SALES AND TASTING:
Weekdays: 08h30 to 17h30
Saturdays: 09h00 to 13h00
Tastings are free of charge.
CELLAR TOURS: Guided cellar tours
are held by appointment.
WINES:
Auret ★★★★ Only 500 cases
containing six bottles each have
been produced from selected

barrels of the 1988 vintage. This
wine, which was released late in
1990, has distinct character. A
bordeaux blend containing some
Merlot will also be launched. Cellar
samples of this vintage promise a
wine of great potential.
Cabernet ★★★★ The first release
from this new Devon Valley cellar
came from the 1988 vintage, and
was released late in 1990 – and only
450 cases at that. The cellar will
specialize in Cabernet and

The homestead at Clos Malverne is framed by the beauty of the Devon Valley. This tiny operation has made a name for itself as a producer of quality wines.

Cabernet blends, with total production not exceeding 4 500 cases. Small quantities have been produced from the 1986 and 1987 vintages, and show great character.

The 1989 has good complexity and is a rich, full-flavoured wine which will develop well.

Pinotage ★★★

DE HELDERBERG CO-OPERATIVE

This is one of the oldest surviving co-ops, having been established way back in 1906. The attractive old building is set close to Winery Road, about one kilometre off the Stellenbosch/Strand road (R44), and is officially in Firgrove. Winery road ends almost at Firgrove station.

Wine maker Inus Muller produces a wide range of popular wines with some most appealing dry reds.

ADDRESS: De Helderberg Co-op, P. O. Box 71, Firgrove 7110
TELEPHONE: (024) 42 2370
FAX: (024) 42 2373
WINE SALES AND TASTING:
Weekdays: 09h00 to 17h30
Saturdays: 09h00 to 16h30
Tastings are free of charge.
CELLAR TOURS: Guided cellar tours take place during the pressing season (January to April) by appointment.
RESTAURANT: Light lunches are served between 12h00 and 14h00, Monday to Saturday, for between R5-75 and R10-00. For large groups, booking is advisable.
WINES:
Cabernet Sauvignon ★★★

Noble Late Harvest ★★★
Vin Rouge ★★★
Blanc de Noir ★★(★)
Chenin Blanc ★★(★)
De Heldere Vonkel ★★★(★)
Pinotage ★★(★)
Shiraz ★★(★)
Cape Riesling ★★
Jerepigo ★★
Late Vintage ★★
Perlé ★★
Pinot Noir ★★
Selected Red ★★
Vin Blanc ★★
Weisser Riesling ★★
Vin Dilue ★
Vin Sucre ★
Sauvignon Blanc (no rating)

DELAIRE

Perched on the top of the Helshoogte pass between Stellenbosch and Franschhoek, this property has some of the highest vineyards in the area. Previously owned by wine-writing wine maker, John Platter, who first bottled in 1985, the farm was purchased by Storm Quinan in 1987. The winery has gone from strength to strength, vintage by vintage. The quality established over three vintages by Mike Dobrovic is now in the talented young hands of Christopher Keet.

A very friendly and personal welcome is always assured in a delightful tasting room with a magnificent view over the Helshoogte valley towards the Groot Drakenstein.

ADDRESS: Delaire Vineyards, P. O. Box 3058, Stellenbosch 7602
TELEPHONE: (02231) 9 1756
FAX: (02231) 9 1270
WINE SALES AND TASTING:
Mondays to Saturdays: 10h00 to 17h00
Wine may be tasted for R1-50, or R5-65 if you buy a glass as well.
CELLAR TOURS: Guided cellar tours may be arranged by appointment.
RESTAURANT: A picnic is offered during the summer months, at R15-00 a head, for which you must book a day in advance. Otherwise, you can simply bring your own picnic and lunch on the lawns in front of the wine-tasting room.

WINES:
Barrique ★★★★ The first release, from the 1988 vintage, is a well-wooded blend of equal proportions of Cabernet and the 1988 Gold Medal SA Champion Merlot. A deep, rich, full-flavoured wine with lots of fruit and good wood, it needs time to soften, but, on the other hand, should age well over eight to 12 years.
Blanc Fumé ★★★★ Left on the lees for at least three weeks after fermentation, a small portion of this attractive, dry wine was wood-aged and underwent malolactic fermentation. The first release by the new management was from the

1988 vintage – a very good, big wine. The 1989 is equally good and full of cultivar character combining with the oak. It is developing very well with time.
Chardonnay ★★★★ The first release from the 1987 showed that this cellar was going to be good for Chardonnay. The 1988 had a good cultivar character with lemon taste and fine wood. The 1989 is a fresher style with the fuller, toffee-type taste, hints of citrus and good wood. It is easy to drink now but has the potential to develop with

benefit in the bottle.
Special Late Harvest ★★★★ This is a delicious, full, fruity wine from the 1989 vintage. It has good botrytis with citrus and tropical fruit notes. Lovely as it is when young, it has potential to develop in the bottle.
Blanc de Noir ★★★(★)
Sauvignon Blanc ★★★(★)
Blanc de Blanc ★★★
Cuvée Rouge ★★★
Grand Cuvée ★★★
Weisser Riesling ★★★
Joie de l'Air ★★

DELHEIM

Spatz Sperling arrived in the Cape in 1951 to work for Mr H. Hoheissen on Delheim. Little could he have imagined that he would develop the property into one of the most important in the area, and that he would become one of the 'characters' of the Cape wine scene. He was also fundamental in establishing the Stellenbosch Wine Route – the Cape's original wine route.

Spatz and Delheim have a history of being a wonderful nursery for talented young wine makers such as Otto Hellman, Kevin Arnold, Jeff Grier, Strorm Kreusch-Dau and Christopher Keet. Right now the cellar is in the competent hands of Philip Costandius who sports the kind of moustache that Delheim's early wine maker, Otto Hellman, did. Philip produces an incredibly good range of wines – apart from his magnificent Cabernets, Grande Reserves, Chardonnays and Late Harvests, there are great value-for-money wines like his Pinotages, Dry Reds and Heerenwijns.

Delheim have a tasting room conducive to good cheer, and a very efficient sales set up. In summer, sitting under a colourful Delheim brolly on the lawn, high up on the Simonsberg foothills looking out over one of the Cape's great views – across the flats to Table Mountain – while sipping delightful Delheim wine and enjoying tasty food must be one of the best ways to spend midday.

ADDRESS: Delheim Wines, P. O. Box 10, Koelenhof 7605
TELEPHONE: (02231) 9 2033
FAX: (02231) 9 2036

Delheim boasts one of the most popular and comfortable tasting rooms in the Cape.

Weekdays: 08h15 to 17h00
Saturdays: 08h30 to 12h00
Wine may be tasted at the following prices: Coupons (five in a booklet) – R1-50 plus tax; tumbler plus coupons – R3-20 plus tax; tulip glass plus coupons – R4-77 plus tax; tumbler – R1-20 plus tax; tulip glass – R3-30 plus tax. The coupons are also valid at Blaauwklippen, Eersterivier, Vlottenburg and Welmoed.

CELLAR TOURS: Guided cellar tours are conducted at 10h00 and 15h00 on weekdays between 1 October and the end of April, and on Saturdays at 10h30 throughout the year.

RESTAURANT: A vintner's platter (from October to the end of April) – one of the better light lunches to be found on the wine route – or country soup (from May to the end of September) is served between 11h00 and 14h00 at R15-00 a head. Booking is essential for groups of more than 10 people.

SHOP: The gift shop sells a variety of souvenirs.

WINES:

Edelspatz Noble Late Harvest ★★★★★ Vintages tasted to date were 1979, 1980, 1981, 1982, 1984, 1987, 1988 and 1989. All were recognizably from the same cellar, but each had its own special distinction. All have definite botrytis character and occasionally have small amounts of Bukettraube or Kerner added to the blend. The 1988 and 1989 have a low sugar content, resulting in a very attractive wine, with good acid balance.

Grand Reserve ★★★★★ This is now firmly established as one of the Cape's great reds. Over its short career, this wine has been acclaimed by critics locally and abroad, and has achieved excellent prices at Independent Winemaker's Guild and Nederberg auctions. It has also been selected as an SAA Wine of the Month and awarded a gold medal at the international Wine and Spirit Competition in 1988. The 1987 has been available since August 1990. Small quantities are bottled in magnums.

Gewürtztraminer ★★★★(★) Always an interesting wine, this is one of the few South African 'traminers which can deservedly be called Gewürtztraminer.

Cabernet Sauvignon ★★★★ One of the Cape's top-quality wine bargains. The 1988 is a very good, complex wine.

Chardonnay ★★★★ The first release, from the 1988 vintage, had high fruit that is now developing well in the bottle. The 1989 vintage is a great improvement with full character, good citrus flavours and buttery, woody backing. It is one of the leading Chardonnays of 1989.

Pinotage Rosé ★★★★ The 1979 was this wine's first vintage and the first Rosé to be certified Superior. An off-dry wine with delightful Pinotage character and an impressive list of show successes, it regularly carries Superior certification.

Shiraz ★★★★ A light South African Shiraz which rounds off beautifully after a year or more in the bottle.

Spatzendreck Late Harvest ★★★★ A semi-sweet wine labelled 'Late Harvest', which, even in the early days, had the character to justify the description. The name and cheeky sparrow featured on the label reflect the lively nature of its wine maker Michael 'Spatz' Sperling.

Special Late Harvest ★★★★ A beautifully flavoured, late harvest wine with a very smooth, palate-pleasing taste. The 1989 is really developing with great benefit.

Blanc Fumé ★★★(★)
Goldspatz Stein ★★★
Heerenwijn ★★★
Pinot Noir ★★★
Pinot Noir Rosé Brut ★★★
Pinotage ★★★
Rhine Riesling ★★★

EERSTERIVIER VALLEISE CO-OPERATIVE

When travelling the R103 from the N2 towards Stellenbosch, you cannot miss the imposing front of this co-op's building, nor their tall-posted entrance, which lies on the left immediately after the road crosses the railway line.

Manie Rossouw, the co-op manager, is an institution in the area and has developed the cellar from an ordinary co-op producing wines for merchants into the attractive complex of today, with its range of bottled varietals. Diners Club winner in 1984 with his Sauvignon Blanc, he regularly has wines on the Nederburg Auction.

As one drives around the Stellenbosch area you will see the corporate signs of the co-op on the farms of its 18 members.

The slopes of the Simonsberg are host to the grapes which produce some of the best red wines in South Africa.

ADDRESS: Eersterivier-Valleise Co-op, P. O. Box 2, Vlottenburg 7604
TELEPHONE: (02231) 9 3870/1
FAX: (02231) 9 3107
WINE SALES AND TASTING:
Weekdays: 08h30 to 12h30 and 13h30 to 17h00
Saturdays: 09h00 to 13h00
Wine may be tasted – a book of five coupons, which is also valid at the Blaauwklippen, Delheim, Vlottenburg and Welmoed wineries, costs R1-70, a tumbler costs R1-70 and a tulip glass costs R4-75.
CELLAR TOURS: Guided tours of the co-operative's wine cellar are held by appointment.
RESTAURANT: Light lunches (R10-00), cheese platters (R6-00), or sausage rolls (R2-50) are served between 11h00 and 14h00 over the Christmas-holiday period (from early December to early January) in the co-operative's wine cellar.
WINES:
Cabernet Sauvignon ★★★
Pinotage ★★★
Riesling ★★★
Sauvignon Blanc ★★★
Special Late Harvest ★★★
Vin Blanc ★★★
Weisser Riesling ★★★
Muscat d'Alexandrie ★★(★)
Chenin Blanc ★★(★)
Shiraz ★★
Vin Rouge ★★

EIKENDAL VINEYARDS

A Swiss-owned operation run by Austrian wine maker Josef Kramer, with South African Jan Boland Coetzee as consultant maker, Eikendal is one of the Cape's most cosmopolitan operations. With a good deal of their production making its way to the Swiss market, the wines of Eikendal have a personality that is perhaps more European than those of many other Cape wineries.

Situated on the Stellenbosch/Somerset West road, on the lower slopes of the Helderberg, the winery was one of the earlier of the modern developments that was built to be attractive as well as functional. The parklike grounds between the dam and the winery make a perfect setting in the summer for their Swiss country lunches. In winter they hold raclette evenings helped along with glasses of warm gluhwein.

An annual, colourful and fun-filled event is their baptizing of the new vintage, which is a festival day held in April each year.

ADDRESS: Eikendal Vineyards,
P. O. Box 2261, Stellenbosch, 7600
TELEPHONE: (024) 55 1422
FAX: (024) 55 1027

WINE SALES AND TASTING:
Weekdays: 09h00 to 17h00
Saturdays: 09h00 to 12h30
Wine may be tasted at a cost of R1-00. A tumbler costs R3-50 and a tulip glass R4-50.
CELLAR TOURS: Guided cellar tours are conducted at 11h30 and 15h30 from December to February, and on request during the rest of the year.
RESTAURANT: A Swiss country lunch is served from Mondays to Fridays between 12h00 and 14h00 from mid-November to mid-April at R16-50 a head. Booking is advisable. In winter (June to September), a Cape winter soup is served for lunch (Mondays to Fridays – 12h00 to 14h00), while a cheese fondue is served on Friday evenings.
SHOP: Some souvenirs are available behind the counter in the wine tasting room.
TOURS: Tractor rides through the vineyards, as well as boat rides, are held during the tourist season (November to February).
OTHER FACILITIES: There is a children's playground on the grounds in front of the winery.
WINES:
Classique ★★★★ From the 1987 vintage, this is a well-wooded blend of 60 per cent Cabernet and 40 per cent Merlot, that will need time to develop.
Cabernet Sauvignon ★★★★ This new cellar made a fine debut with the blending of a small amount of Shiraz, giving its Cabernets greater complexity and the potential to develop well. The 1987 will need time to settle.
Special Late Harvest ★★★(★)
Sauvignon Blanc ★★★
Blanc de Blanc ★★★
Cabernet Reserve du Patron ★★★
Duc de Berry Rouge ★★★
Pinot Noir ★★★
Blanc Cuvée ★★(★)
Duc de Berry C'est si Blanc ★★
Duc de Berry Late Harvest ★★
Duc de Berry Stein ★★
Duc de Berry Premier Grand Crû (no rating)

HARTENBERG

Hartenberg Estate, was for many years known as Montagne and was originally part of the farm Nooitgedacht, granted to an ancestor of the Esterhuizen family named Christoffel Estreux in 1704. The winery has now settled down, after a number of changes of ownership and ideas of management, into a very dedicated quality venture. It is owned by international businessman Ken Mackenzie, who has in charge bachelor wine maker, Danie Truter.

The well-aged reds of the property are almost legend, and tend to overshadow the very good whites.

ADDRESS: Hartenberg Estate,
P. O. Box 69, Koelenhof 7605
TELEPHONE: (02231) 9 2541
FAX: (02231) 9 2268
WINE SALES AND TASTING:
Weekdays: 08h00 to 17h00
Saturdays: 08h00 to 16h00
Wine may be tasted; there is no charge.
CELLAR TOURS: Guided cellar tours are held at 10h00 and 15h00 on weekdays, and at 10h00 on Saturdays throughout the year.
RESTAURANT: A lunch is served between 12h00 and 14h00 at R15-00 a head. From October to the end of April, this takes the form of a very good vintner's lunch – enjoyed outdoors in the park surrounds and close to the new underground maturation cellar – while from May to the end of September a soup is served.
WINES:
L'Estreux ★★★★ L'Estreux is only bottled in those vintages when the cellar believes that nature has provided the style of wine that fits their quality requirement. The 1989 is 40 per cent Chenin Blanc with the balance made up from Gewürztraminer, Morio Muscat and others. It has a nice touch of botrytis, but not enough to cover the fresh, fruity, Muscat character.
Shiraz ★★★★ The first release was a very good wine from the 1979 vintage. It was full of cultivar character and is still developing. All Hartenberg's Shirazes carry the Superior certification.
Cabernet Sauvignon ★★★(★)
Premium Blend ★★★(★)
Bin 3 ★★★
Bin 6 ★★★
Bin 9 ★★★
Blanc de Noir ★★★
Weisser Riesling ★★★
Zinfandel ★★★
Chatillon ★★(★)
Sauvignon Blanc ★★(★)

The homestead and outbuildings of Morgenhof were built in 1820. The farm has had a chequered history, but today it is one of the attractions of the Stellenbosch Wine Route.

MORGENHOF

On the Klapmuts road (R44) about four kilometres from Stellenbosch, almost opposite the Wine Route Hotel, is an historic farm dating back to 1692 that has undergone expensive restoration and redevelopment to make it one of the Cape's showpieces. The estate is owned by some Johannesburg-based, German businessmen, whose intention it is to have Morgenhof as a top winery and tourist attraction that will boast one of the best restaurants in the country. The buildings have been fully restored, though not all back to their original purpose. Where the stables were, for example, you can now enjoy a farm lunch, and the original cellar is now the barrel-maturation cellar.

Pietie Theron, the retired KWV wine maestro, acts as consultant to the wine maker, young Denzil van Vuuren, while Margie Hare doubles as marketing manager for the winery and herb specialist. She has developed a large and commercially viable herb garden, boasting more than 60 different kinds of herb, which not only makes an interesting attraction for visitors to stroll through at leisure, but will provide the estate's restaurant with all the herbs the chef will ever be likely to require.

ADDRESS: Morgenhof, P. O. Box 365, Stellenbosch 7600
TELEPHONE: (02231) 9 5510
FAX: (02231) 9 5266
WINE SALES AND TASTING:
Weekdays: 09h00 to 16h30
Saturdays: 09h00 to 15h30
Wine may be tasted at a cost of R2-00 plus tax, or R3-50 plus tax if you buy a glass as well.

CELLAR TOURS: There are no cellar tours, but a special platform allows views of the cellar.
RESTAURANT: In summer (October to April), you may buy a picnic basket – to picnic in the garden – at R15-00 a head, while in winter (May to September), soup, pâté and bread are served at R10-00 a head. Booking for groups is essential.
HISTORICAL ATTRACTIONS: Visitors may wander through the historic buildings of the estate. Morgenhof also boasts a museum cellar, where, during the pressing season (February and March), visitors can see how wine was made during the 19th Century. Only group bookings are accepted for this.
TOURS: At 11h15 every day, there is a drive to 'Champagne Corner' which offers 360° views of the surrounding areas. This is for

groups only, and they must book.
WINES:
Cabernet Sauvignon ★★★★ The 1984 Cabernet is Morgenhof's first release. They couldn't have picked a better vintage with which to begin. A deep-coloured, well-balanced wine with fine character backed with good wood, it has enough tannin to develop well with time. There was no release of the 1985 vintage, but the 1986 is available – a lighter wine which tastes good now and probably won't age as long as the 1984 vintage.
Ruby Port (Pieties Port) ★★★(★)
Sauvignon Blanc ★★★
Chenin Blanc ★★(★)
Blanc de Blanc ★★
Blanc de Noir ★★
Rhine Riesling ★★
Chenin Blanc Special Late Harvest (no rating)

Trees surround the homestead at Muratie. The name – from the Dutch word murasie, *meaning 'ruins' – was given by Georg Canitz when he came across the near-derelict farm in 1925.*

MURATIE

To get to Delheim, you have to drive through the historic Muratie Estate. Muratie was long owned by Annemarie Canitz, daughter of German immigrant Georg Canitz, and has been recently purchased by Ronnie Melck, formerly managing director of Stellenbosch Farmers' Winery. He has undertaken massive redevelopment of the vineyards, and will specialize in producing red wines.

The famous old buildings will be repaired, but kept as close to their well-known appearance as possible. A major change in the cellar is the introduction of new French-oak barrels.

ADDRESS: Muratie Estate,
P. O. Box 9, Koelenhof 7605
TELEPHONE: (02231) 9 2330
WINE SALES AND TASTING:
Mondays to Thursdays: 09h00 to 17h00
Fridays: 09h00 to 16h00
Saturdays: 09h00 to 13h00
Wine may be tasted for R2-50 (a glass is included in the price).
CELLAR TOURS: No cellar tours.
SHOP: A shop on the estate sells souvenirs.

WINES:
Port ★★★
Amber ★★
Cabernet Sauvignon ★★
Claret ★★
Pinot Noir ★★
Red Velvet ★★
Dry White ★
Dry White No. 2 ★
Stein ★
Special Dry Red ★

NEETHLINGSHOF

This is an old and well-established farm (it was granted by Simon van der Stel to Willem Barend Lubbe in the 1600's), previously owned by well-known local personality, Jannie Momberg, but bought by international banker, Hans Joachim Schreiber, in 1985. He replanted the vineyards, refurbished the cellars and totally transformed the property into a showpiece winery/vineyard of the Cape. The farm employees' village is a model of modern development and the various tourist facilities are the best imaginable.

The wines to date have been patchy, with an outstanding Cabernet in 1983, made by Gyles Webb. With Günter Brözel now in charge, though, this cellar is destined to produce some of the Cape's most exciting wines. Freed from producing the styles of wine he had made Nederburg famous for, Günter has already shown, in two vintages, young wines of modern world class, and won the Jan Smuts Trophy for South Africa's Grand Champion wine in 1990 with a Noble Late Harvest Rhine Riesling, which is a style in which we all know he is a specialist. However, his modern wooded Chardonnays and his young reds are going to be the wines of the future.

Neethlingshof is a must to visit.

ADDRESS: Neethlingshof,
P. O. Box 104, Stellenbosch 7600
TELEPHONE: (02231) 7 6532
FAX: (02231) 7 8171

WINE SALES AND TASTING:
Weekdays: 09h00 to 17h00
Saturdays: 10h00 to 16h00
Tastings cost R7-00 a head.

Though Neethlingshof has been totally rejuvenated in recent years, the gracious old manor house has been preserved.

CELLAR TOURS: Guided cellar tours are conducted every hour on the hour from December to February, and at 11h30 and 15h30 for the rest of the year. Groups of up to 80 people can organize tours by prior arrangement.

RESTAURANT: The Lord Neethling Restaurant serves Chinese and Continental dishes of a level unmatched in the Cape (though they are somewhat pricey), and is open for lunch (Tuesday to Sunday – 12h00 to 15h00) and dinner (Tuesday to Saturday – 19h00 to 22h30). It is advisable to book.

From November to April, light lunches and afternoon teas are served outdoors on the (less expensive) Palm Terrace. Bookings are not taken.

OTHER FACILITIES: Neethlingshof boasts conference facilities for up to 75 people, and a playground for children.

WINES:

Gewürztraminer Special Late Harvest ★★★★ A well-made wine from the 1984 vintage, with excellent cultivar character. It has developed beautifully in the bottle.

Weisser Riesling Special Late Harvest ★★★★ The maiden vintage was 1983: a beautiful wine with complexity which can only come from botrytis and good wine-making. It has deservedly been awarded Superior certification and is developing well in the bottle.

Cabernet Sauvignon ★★★(★)
Frülingwein ★★★(★)
Gewürztraminer ★★★(★)
Lord Neethling Rouge ★★★(★)
Weisser Riesling ★★★(★)
Blanc de Noir ★★★
Colombar ★★★

Neethlingshoffer ★★★
Pinotage ★★★
Riesling ★★★

Bukettraube ★★(★)
Sauvignon Blanc ★★
Rhine Riesling (no rating)

OUDE NEKTAR

Oude Nektar Wine Estate is owned by Hans Peter Schroder, who went to school at Paul Roos in Stellenbosch, worked 23 years in Japan, has business interests in California, and is now putting all his effort, through wine maker Peter Peck, into developing Oude Nektar into one of the Cape's top producers.

Situated in one of the most beautiful valleys in the Cape, Jonkershoek, Oude Nektar will be well worth visiting once their redevelopment programme is complete.

ADDRESS: Oude Nektar, P. O. Box 389, Stellenbosch 7600
TELEPHONE: (02231) 7 0690
FAX: (02231) 7 0647
WINE SALES AND TASTING:
Weekdays: 09h30 to 17h00
Saturdays: 11h00 to 16h00

Wines may be tasted for R1-00.
CELLAR TOURS: There are no cellar tours.
RESTAURANT: Between 15 December and 15 January, a picnic lunch may be bought (R15-00 plus tax) which you can enjoy on the

lawns under the trees. Booking is essential.

WINES:

Furmint ★★★★ The first release was the 1983, one of the earliest Cape wines to carry the name of this Hungarian variety. The 1986 deserves four stars, but the 1987 is not as good.

Cabernet Sauvignon ★★★(★)
Blanc de Noir ★★★
La Bouquet Blanc ★★★
Olasz Riesling ★★★
Shiraz ★★★
Special Late Vintage ★★★
Pinotage ★★(★)

OVERGAAUW

Although the Overgaauw winery and pretty Victorian sales-and-tasting facility are situated at the lower end of the Stellenbosch Kloof their vineyards stretch high up onto the cool hills behind. The Van Veldens are one of the longest established wine families of the area, with direct descendancy going back 80 years (Abraham Julius van Velden bought the farm from his maternal grandfather, Willem Joubert, in 1906). They have also been leaders in the production of quality wines and, having bottled some of their own production since 1970, were amongst the earliest to do so. They were leaders in the fields of using new, small, French-oak barriques to mature their Cabernet, producing Bordeaux-style blends and experimenting with other interesting dry-red blends – of which their Overtinto (a blend of Portuguese varieties) has become a popular change of flavour from the many Cabernet-based wines in the Cape.

Apart from their great reds – including a Merlot – they have always been fine producers of white wines – of which their Sylvaner has a special place, being the only wine in the Cape to be produced from this grape. It has the most unusual keeping and development ability.

When one talks of Overgaauw, mention must be made of their Port. Long time producers using the traditional Port varieties, they produce a wine that can easily be mistaken for one originating from Portugal. Made from the same five varietals as the Overtinto, Overgaauw Port is an obligatory acquisition if you want to be considered half way to having a good Cape cellar.

ADDRESS: Overgaauw Estate, P. O. Box 3, Vlottenburg 7604
TELEPHONE: (02231) 9 3815
FAX: (02231) 9 3436

WINE SALES AND TASTING:
Weekdays: 08h30 to 12h30 and 14h00 to 17h00
Saturdays: 10h00 to 12h30
Tastings are free of charge.
CELLAR TOURS: Guided cellar tours are held every Wednesday at 14h30, otherwise by appointment.

WINES:

Tria Corda ★★★★★ A red blend that will be a wine to watch in vintages to come. The 1981 comprises 70 per cent Cabernet Sauvignon, with Merlot providing the balance. The estate has made good individual wines from these cultivars, and now, in blending and good oak ageing, seems to have brought out the best in both, resulting in one of the Cape's most promising wines. The 1985 and 1986 are 65 per cent Cabernet Sauvignon, 20 per cent Cabernet Franc, and 15 per cent Merlot. So far all the vintages have developed well.

Cabernet Sauvignon ★★★★(★) One of South Africa's consistently good Cabernets, with no less than seven vintages of the 1970s receiving the Superior certification. The wine has an unmistakable cellar characteristic on the nose, and good wood treatment which complements the Cabernet without overwhelming it. An excellent wine made from some of South Africa's best Cabernet grapes, it is known to mature with rare distinction over 10 years or more.

Chardonnay ★★★★(★) The 1986 was a rich and full-flavoured wine, and the 1987 is even better, having a very good combination of cultivars and wood. The 1989 has toffee and butterscotch flavours and is the best to date.

Overtinto ★★★★ A very good blend of Port varieties, including Tinta Barocca. This is one of the more unusual South African red wines, tasting, not surprisingly, like a dry Port. It is full-bodied and ages well.

Port ★★★★ This Port, made from various cultivars, has been wood-aged for two years and then bottled in the true Vintage Port style. It develops well, but needs many years to reach its full potential.

Merlot ★★★(★)
Sauvignon Blanc ★★★(★)
Sylvaner ★★★(★)

RUST-EN-VREDE

One of the three estates at the end of the Helderberg that has ex-Springbok rugby players as wine makers or owners. In this case, the flying blonde winger of the 1960s, Jannie Engelbrecht, is the owner, and was the original wine maker when bottling began in 1979. Today, and in fact since 1987, he has been joined by champion specialist red-wine maker, Kevin Arnold.

From producing a range of reds, they have now decided to concentrate their production on four wines and specialize in Cabernet-based or Claret-type wines. They already produce some of the Cape's best, but are working tirelessly to do better, and putting considerable cash and effort behind achieving their goal.

South Africans both, they refer to their blends as Stellenbosch blends and make no mention of France, although top Bordeaux quality is their aim. Having said that, they produce a superb Shiraz and their Tinta Barocca is probably the most attractive wine in the Cape made from this variety.

Rust-en-Vrede is a delightful property to visit, with lovely old Cape Dutch buildings standing out in front of a tastefully built modern cellar facility. The tasting room is well organized, and looks into the cellar area giving the feel of tasting right in the birthplace of the wine.

To get there, take the Annandale road towards the Helderberg, and then look for the signs to the left.

ADDRESS: Rust-en-Vrede, P. O. Box 473, Stellenbosch 7600
TELEPHONE: (02231) 9 3881/3757
FAX: (02231) 9 3000
WINE SALES AND TASTING:
Weekdays: 08h30 to 12h30 and 13h30 to 16h30
Saturdays: 09h00 to 12h00
Tastings are free of charge.
CELLAR TOURS: Guided cellar tours are held on request.

WINES:

Cabernet Sauvignon ★★★★ The estate's maiden vintage Cabernet (1979) was good, but succeeding ones were disappointing, and the critics were quick to claim beginner's luck. The 1982 is, however, an exceptionally good wine. I thought that the 1984 was probably the best that far of the 1980s, but the 1986 is even better and the 1987 will also be great. All vintages carry Superior certification.

Shiraz ★★★★ The 1979 was an outstanding wine with full flavour,

Harvesting usually takes place in the cool hours of the morning, so that the sun's heat does not spoil the grapes.

which has developed well in the bottle. The 1986 is a lovely, big, tasty wine, and the 1987 is big, bold and full-flavoured.

Tinta Barocca ★★★(★)
Pinot Noir ★★★

SAXENBURG

This estate is now going by its original name, and not 'Saxenheim', which it used until recently as Bertrams had the rights to the name Saxenburg. The new Swiss owners, Henry and Silvia Harrer and Adrian and Brigitte Bührer came to an amicable arrangement with Bertrams, allowing them to use the property's original name on their wine labels.

A visit to the property will illustrate how well the vineyards are situated to benefit from the cooling breezes from both False Bay and Table Bay. Situated at the western end of the Bottelary hills and overlooking Kuilsrivier, they are busy being reworked, and more Cabernet Sauvignon and Cabernet Franc are being planted, as well as new plantings such as Chardonnay and Merlot.

The owners are busy restoring the farm's historic buildings which will house a restaurant. Saxenburg is easy to reach, being on the Polkadraai Road (R306), which links Stellenbosch to Kuilsrivier.

ADDRESS: Saxenburg, P. O. Box 171, Kuilsrivier 7580
TELEPHONE: (021) 903 6113
FAX: (021) 903 3129
WINE SALES AND TASTING:
Weekdays: 08h00 to 17h00
Saturdays: 09h00 to 16h00
Wine may be tasted: tastings cost R1-00 a head.
CELLAR TOURS: There are no cellar tours.

WINES:
Noble Late Harvest ★★★★ This is a full, fruity-flavoured wine with a most attractive nose.
Special Late Harvest ★★★(★)
Blanc de Blanc ★★★
Sauvignon Blanc ★★★
Blanc de Noir ★★(★)
Pinotage ★★(★)
Chenin Blanc (no rating)
Perlé Pére Francis (no rating)

SIMONSIG

The actual Simonsig winery is on the M23, the road that links the Stellenbosch/Klapmuts road with the Stellenbosch/Koelenhof road. However, their vineyards cover a much wider area, allowing them to grow different varieties on sites better suited to them than those in the immediate vicinity of the winery.

Frans Malan, the owner, was a prime mover in getting the Stellenbosch Wine Route established and, as such, has always ensured good facilities to cater for the large numbers of visitors to Simonsig. Frans has always been highly innovative and extremely energetic in promoting his product, and has been at the forefront of development in all that is good for the industry. Nowadays, the operation is run by father and sons, with vineyards, orchards and vegetables being looked after by Francois, wine making by Johan and marketing by Pieter.

For years Simonsig wines have been award winners in all kinds of shows and competitions – locally and overseas – over a wide spectrum of styles and types of wine. However, 1990 must have brought special satisfaction to the team; Johan collected no less than three trophies at the International Wine and Spirit Competition award ceremony at the Guildhall in London. He was only points away from being the International Winemaker of the Year, an award only once gained by a South African (Günter Brözel back in 1986). Johan was inched out by a Californian who had been in Johan's position on no fewer than four occasions in the past six years! So there is still hope for Johan.

At that competition he received the Cape Wine Academy trophy for the best South African white wine with his 1988 Reserve Chardonnay and the Dave Hughes Trophy for the best South African red wine for his 1984 Reserve Cabernet. This was the first time that the Dave Hughes Trophy had been awarded. He also won the Packaging Trophy for his wine dressed in the Cape Independent Winemaker's Guild livery.

The Stellenbosch mountains provide a backdrop to the vineyards at Rust-en-Vrede, as well as to their gardens of roses and cannas.

Apart from the wines winning International acclaim, Simonsig have a range of wines suited to satisfy almost any palate, with exceptional Late Harvests and nine years of Superior certifications for their Gewürztraminers. Their Kaapse Vonkel led the Cape's resurgence of producing *méthode champenoise*, and, in recent years, has been amongst the best produced in the Cape.

ADDRESS: Simonsig Estate, P. O. Box 6, Koelenhof 7605
TELEPHONE: (02231) 9 2443/2044
FAX: (02231) 9 2545
WINE SALES AND TASTING:
Weekdays: 08h00 to 17h00
Saturdays: 08h00 to 12h30
Wines may be tasted for R3-00 plus tax (glass and tasting).
CELLAR TOURS: Guided cellar tours take place during harvest time (January to March) at 10h00 and 15h00 – otherwise by appointment.
SHOP: A 'Snuffelwinkel' sells souvenirs and home-made produce.
WINES:
Chardonnay ★★★★(★) After an indifferent start in 1980 and 1981, the 1982 vintage obtained a Superior certification. With its very good nose and fair flavour, this wine gained acclaim at a tasting in Spain arranged by the world authority, Miguel Torres, competing very successfully with good Chardonnays from around the world. The 1989 has a good fruity nose and fine caramel and toffee flavours. It will develop well over five to seven years.
Gewürztraminer ★★★★ This wine appeared for the first time out of the 1977 vintage, and was sold at the Nederburg Auction. It possesses the rose-petal nose associated with the variety, and has now developed a reputation as one of the Cape's best Gewürztraminers, a good, full, rich, sweet wine, full of cultivar character, and almost always Superior.
Morio Muscat ★★★★ A most attractive, award-winning,

1988 is not as big as the 1987 but should develop well. These are most attractive wines that age with benefit.

Cabernet Sauvignon ★★★(★)
Colombard ★★★(★)
Kaapse Vonkel ★★★(★)
Pinot Noir ★★★(★)
Sauvignon Blanc ★★★(★)
Shiraz ★★★(★)
Vin Fumé ★★★(★)
Adelberg ★★★

Blanc de Noir ★★★
Chenin Blanc ★★★
Franciskaner Special Late Harvest ★★★
Mustique ★★★
Pinotage ★★★
Riesling ★★★
Sonstein ★★★
Muscat Ottonel ★★(★)
Mistelle ★★
Rosé ★★
Primeur (no rating)

SPIER

Spier is one of the Stellenbosch Wine Route's foundation members, and over the years their venue between Lynedoch and Stellenbosch has grown into one of the major attractions of the area. When opened to the public, the complex of old Cape Dutch buildings housed a restaurant, in the old slave quarters, and a sales-office-cum-tasting-room. Today, alongside the old homestead, a highly successful Jonkershuis dining area has been established where one can sit under the oaks or inside and enjoy lighter lunches of cheese boards, pâtés etc. There is also an art school and art gallery well worth visiting. The actual winery is tucked away in the Stellenbosch Kloof.

The buildings under the oaks that form the Spier public area cannot be missed as they have four tall flags alongside the R310, which will attract your attention as they are a unique design in the winelands.

ADDRESS: Spier Estate, P. O. Box 28, Vlottenburg 7604
TELEPHONE: (02231) 9 3808/9
FAX: (02231) 9 3514
WINE SALES AND TASTING: Sales Weekdays: 08h30 to 17h00
Saturdays: 08h30 to 13h00

Wine tasting takes place from 08h30 to 16h30 on weekdays and from 08h30 to 12h30 on Saturdays. A booklet of five coupons (one coupon per tasting) costs R2-50, a tumbler R1-85, and a tulip glass R4-55.

semi-sweet wine with very enticing nose. It is something of a limited release, but is well worth searching for. The 1988 was judged South African Champion.

Noble Late Harvest ★★★★ This wine was first produced in 1979 from Steen and Bukettraube, and was light in all respects. The 1982 won a gold medal at the South African Championship Wine Show and is a most attractive wine of interesting complexity and deep richness. The 1983 and 1984 are much lighter and more delicate, with lovely fruity noses and flavours. The latter is still on sale but cellar samples show the continuing high standard one has come to expect from this wine.

Weisser Riesling ★★★★ Weisser Riesling has become a speciality of this estate. It appeared for the first time with the 1977 vintage and was sold as a rare wine at the 1978 Nederburg Auction. It has developed with subsequent vintages. The 1986 and 1987 vintages are both Superior. The

Wine is drawn from small casks with a wine thief at Simonsig – every barrel is constantly checked for quality.

Spier is one the oldest farms in the Stellenbosch area, having been granted to Arnout Jansz in 1692. The old slave house is now a restaurant.

CELLAR TOURS: Guided cellar tours are held at 11h00, Mondays to Fridays, throughout the year.
RESTAURANT: The Spier Restaurant, which specializes in Cape cooking, serves lunches between 12h00 and 15h30 Thursday to Sunday, and suppers on Fridays and Saturdays (from 19h00). Booking is essential during the tourist season.
The Jonkershuis serves light lunches (cheese platters, pâtés etc.) daily between 12h00 and 15h30, as well as teas (09h00 to 11h30 and 15h00 to 16h30 daily).
SHOP: Some souvenirs can be bought at the wine-tasting room.
OTHER FACILITIES: The Ou Kelder Art Gallery (as the name suggests, an old wine cellar converted into an art gallery) is open from 10h00 to 16h30, Mondays to Saturdays. On the first Saturday of each month (09h00 to 16h00), Spier hosts the Somerset-West craft market.
WINES:
Colombar Special Late Harvest ★★★★(★) The Superior 1979 is one of the most interesting botrytis wines. The 1985 was a fruity, well-made wine, which has developed with time.
Chenin Blanc Special Late Harvest ★★★(★)
Edelsteen Late Harvest ★★★(★)
Cabernet Sauvignon ★★★
Noble Late Harvest ★★★
Pinotage ★★★
Riesling ★★★
Shiraz ★★★
Clos des Oliviers ★★(★)
Durendal Rosé ★★(★)
Premier Grand Crû ★★(★)
Blanc de Blanc ★★
Blanc de Noir ★★
Bukettraube ★★
Durendal Red ★★
Mistelle ★★
Port ★★
Sauvignon Blanc ★★
Vin Brut ★★
Vin Doux ★★
Vin Rouge ★★
Vin Sec ★★
Bouquet Blanc (no rating)
Gewürztraminer Late Harvest (no rating)
Special Late Harvest (no rating)
Vin du Chêne (no rating)

UITERWYK

Virtually as far up the Stellenbosch Kloof as you can go in a car brings you to the gracious Uiterwyk homestead. Danie de Waal began bottling the wines he had been making and supplying to merchants back in 1972, when that was a not altogether usual practice. Today, wine making is shared by two of his sons, Daniel and Chris, while a graduate in economics, third son Pieter, heads the marketing.

The estate has been in the family since 1682, when the land was settled by Dirk Coetzee – it was formerly granted to him in 1699 by Willem Adriaan van der Stel. The current brothers are the fifth generation to make wine here. The cellar, built in 1798, is still in use – although considerably enlarged and obviously much modernized – and epitomizes the quiet, gentle, reserved manner of the De Waals and their wines.

ADDRESS: Uiterwyk Estate, P. O. Box 15, Vlottenburg 7604
TELEPHONE: (02231) 9 3711
FAX: (02231) 9 3776
WINE SALES AND TASTING:
Mondays to Saturdays: 08h30 to 16h30
Tastings are free of charge.
CELLAR TOURS: From February to the beginning of April, guided cellar tours are held at 11h00 and 15h00 – otherwise on request.
WALKS: There is a walk of approximately one and a half kilometres through the farm's vineyards.
WINES:
Cabernet Sauvignon ★★★(★)
Bukettraube ★★★
Estate Sauvignon Blanc ★★★
Merlot ★★★
Riesling ★★★
Müller-Thurgau ★★(★)
Weisser Riesling ★★(★)
Colombar ★★
Pinotage ★★
Blanc de Noir (no rating)
Kromhout (no rating)

VLOTTENBURG CO-OPERATIVE

Directly opposite the Vlottenburg station, separated from it by the R103, is a co-op established in 1945. Kowie du Toit, the wine maker, is a very modest man and tends to sell his wine at very modest prices. The result is some of the best value-for-money wines around. Kowie's first attempt at Chardonnay (1990) is way better than most other co-ops have managed – in fact, better than a lot of non co-operative cellars.

ADDRESS: Vlottenburg Co-op,
P. O. Box 40, Vlottenburg 7604
TELEPHONE: (02231) 9 3828/9
WINE SALES AND TASTING:
Weekdays: 08h30 to 17h00
Saturdays: 09h00 to 12h30
Tasting costs R2-90 for a tumbler and coupons – coupons also valid at Blaauwklippen, Delheim, Eersterivier and Welmoed.
CELLAR TOURS: Guided cellar tours are held from December to February at 10h30 and 15h30.
WINES:
Cabernet Sauvignon ★★★

Chenin Blanc ★★★
Gewürztraminer ★★★
Riesling ★★★
Special Late Harvest ★★★
Steen ★★★
Weisser Riesling ★★★
Hanepoot ★★(★)
Muscat de Hambourg ★★(★)
Gamay ★★
Pinotage ★★
Premier Grand Crû ★★
Sauvignon Blanc ★★
Blanc de Blanc ★
Chardonnay (no rating)

VREDENHEIM

Vredenheim has been producing wines for many years, but only when it was purchased by Coen Bezuidenhout in 1986 did commercial bottling become a consideration. At that time, the farm's name was Vredenburg, but as that name was a long-time brand name of Gilbeys, the Bezuidenhout's could not use it – so they settled for Vredenheim.

Vredenheim is easy to find as you head towards Stellenbosch along the R103: turn right a few hundred metres after passing Vlottenburg station and the Van Rhyn Distillery on your right, and the Vlottenburg Co-op on the left. BEWARE the unguarded railway level crossing.

ADDRESS: Vredenheim Estate Wines, P. O. Box 369, Stellenbosch 7600

TELEPHONE: (02231) 9 3637/3878
WINE SALES AND TASTING:
Weekdays: 09h00 to 16h30

Saturdays: 09h00 to 12h00
Wine may be tasted at a cost of 50c per tasting, but the money will be refunded if you buy of the wine that you have tasted.
CELLAR TOURS: Guided cellar tours are held on request.

WINES:
Blanc de Noir ★★★
Cabernet Sauvignon ★★★
Chenin Blanc (no rating)
Colombar (no rating)
Debuut Wit Tafelwyn (no rating)
Weisser Riesling (no rating)

WELMOED CO-OPERATIVE

In 1991 this co-op celebrated 50 years of existence. This is the first co-op you come to on the R103 when travelling from Cape Town to Stellenbosch. Set back on the right hand side, the winery is right on the banks of the Eerste River.

ADDRESS: Welmoed Co-op,
P. O. Box 23, Lynedoch 7603
TELEPHONE: (02231) 9 3800/1
FAX: (02231) 9 3434
WINE SALES AND TASTING:
Mondays to Saturdays: 08h30 to 17h00
Wine tasting costs R1-70 for a booklet of five coupons (one tasting per coupon), and R2-00 for a glass. The coupons are also valid at Blaauwklippen, Delheim, Eersterivier and Vlottenburg.
CELLAR TOURS: Guided cellar tours are held by appointment during most of the year, and on request during harvest time (January to March).
RESTAURANT: From 1 October to the end of April, a picnic lunch is served either inside the cellar or outside (at tables or on the lawns) at R15-00 a head.

WINES:
Noble Late Harvest ★★★★ Made from Steen, the 1983 vintage has a burnt-gold colour, good attractive nose and full flavour. It developed beautifully in the bottle and now needs drinking.
Fortified Wines ★★★
Fortified Muscat Wines ★★★
Riesling ★★★
Rouge Sec ★★★
Sauvignon Blanc ★★★
Shiraz ★★★
Special Late Harvest ★★★
Vintage Port ★★★
Weisser Riesling ★★★
Pinotage ★★(★)
Blanc de Noir ★★
Chenin Blanc ★★
Cuvée Brut ★★
Grand Crû ★★
Late Vintage ★★
Zinfandel ★★

The Helderberg and the Stellenbosch Mountains rise up behind the cellars of the Welmoed Co-op. Originally, Welmoed was a farm granted to Henning Huysing in 1690.

ALPHEN

Alphen is a name with a long history in South African wine, dating back to the days of Simon van der Stel, when the original Alphen farm in Constantia was part of the extensive properties owned by the Governor. In 1712, when Van der Stel died, Alphen was granted to Theunis Dirkz by the Dutch East India Company, and in 1850 it was bought by the Cloete family.

The growth of Cape Town forced Alphen to move its base, and in 1972, Gilbeys bought the brand, and established a winery on the farm of Kleine Zalze. This farm is situated on the R44, a few kilometres out of Stellenbosch, at the same turnoff as that of the Technopark.

The cellar draws its grapes from a number of farms in the area best suited to a particular variety.

ADDRESS: Klein Zalze, P. O. Box 137, Stellenbosch 7600
TELEPHONE: (02231) 7 5036
FAX: (02231) 9 9430
WINE SALES AND TASTING: By appointment only.

BERGKELDER

Cut deep into the southern slopes of the Papegaaiberg is a magnificent cellar that is home to many of South Africa's finest wines. Stellenryck, Fleur du Cap and J C le Roux are made here, and the wines of most of the estates in the Bergkelder scheme are blended, matured and bottled on the premises. Visitors can take guided tours of the underground cellars, see the Vinotec stocks maturing and inspect the beautifully carved vats. Wine tastings are held by candlelight in the cellars.

ADDRESS: Bergkelder, Private Bag X5001, Stellenbosch 7600
TELEPHONE: (02231) 7 3480
WINE SALES AND TASTING: No cellar sales.
For tastings see 'Cellar tours'.
CELLAR TOURS: Guided cellar tours, including tastings, are held Mondays to Saturdays at 10h00 and 15h00 at R5-00 a head. Booking is essential.
WINES:
Meerlust Cabernet Sauvignon ★★★★★ The Meerlust Cabernet Sauvignon has a superb reputation, and justifiably so. A fine wine, it is lighter-bodied and stylish. All releases have been certified Superior. A feature of the Meerlust Cabernets is their complex nose and excellent flavour, set off by the judicious use of new wood. It is not surprising, then, that they have been consistent winners at young wine shows, judged more than once to be South African champion.
Meerlust Rubicon ★★★★★ This is an excellent blend of Cabernet Sauvignon, Cabernet Franc and Merlot. The first vintage was 1980: a lovely, soft, full-flavoured wine of great complexity, which is developing well in the bottle. The 1985 is exceptionally good for the vintage, while the 1986 is the best to date.
Stellenryck Collection Cabernet Sauvignon ★★★★★ The 1986 is a beautiful, big deep-flavoured wine that will need years to show its true potential.
Fleur du Cap Cabernet Sauvignon ★★★★(★) These are always good, medium-bodied, elegant Cabernets with good varietal noses. They are well balanced, with clean, full Cabernet character which makes pleasant drinking when relatively young, yet they always have the potential to age well.
Le Bonheur Cabernet Sauvignon ★★★★(★) It seems that whenever Michael Woodhead sets out to make a wine, he does so with distinction. The 1984 vintage of this wine is the best one so far. Deep and full-flavoured, it has lots of fruit and fine wood, giving great complexity.
L'Ormarins Blanc Fumé ★★★★(★) A wine packed with powerful cultivar nose and flavour, touched out beautifully with good oak. This Blanc Fumé is consistently one of South Africa's best.

Middelvlei Cabernet Sauvignon ★★★★(★) The 1981 vintage was the first release of a Cabernet from this estate, and it won gold medals at the Stellenbosch and South African Championship shows. The 1984 is a big powerful wine that will develop over many years.
Mont Blois White Muscadel ★★★★(★) A consistent award winner at home and abroad, this rich delicious, golden-coloured dessert wine is the classic of Robertson Muscadels. It might develop in the bottle, but is so good when released that I think that's the time to enjoy it. There are a 1985 and a 1987 to be found.
Rietvallei Red Muscadel ★★★★(★) A sweet fortified wine of the kind every South African should try, as an alternative to after-dinner Port – it's excellent. The wine is vintage dated and is a Wine of Origin Robertson. The 1985 is particularly attractive. It is always Superior and is really what this cellar does best.
Uitkyk Carlonet ★★★★(★) Deserving though it is of its Superior rating, this wine is very different from the Carlonets of old. If judged as a modern Carlonet, however, it will be satisfying enough. Today's Uitkyk Carlonets taste seductively ready at an early age, but deceptively so, for they need some time to fulfil their true potential. The 1986 is a soft, pleasant wine with good cultivar flavours and nice oak.
Aan de Wagenweg Blanc Fumé ★★★★ This is produced in very small quantities. The first release came from the 1989 vintage and was launched early in 1990. This wine was made from grapes grown in the Stellenbosch district and was aged for six months in small oak, and then in the bottle for another six months, before release. It is a pale colour with a good varietal nose backed by nice oak. It should develop well in the bottle through to the mid-1990s.
Aan de Wagenweg Chardonnay ★★★★ This is produced in very small quantities. The first release was from the 1988 vintage and was launched early in 1990. Made from grapes grown in the Durbanville district, the wine is fermented in the barrel and aged on the lees for a year. It is then bottle-aged for another 12 months. It has lots of fruit and a lovely pear-drop nose that is backed with good oak.
Allesverloren Cabernet Sauvignon ★★★★ Until the 1982 vintage, this was usually full-bodied Cabernet made in the traditional manner. Thereafter there was a difference in style, with the prominence of new oak. The 1986 is a fine, big, complex wine with good oak.
Allesverloren Port ★★★★ A consistent and highly successful Port with many Superior certifications and young-wine-show medals and trophies to its credit. It is made predominantly of Tinta Barocca, with the balance comprising Suzão, giving a deep rich, ruby Port which ranks among the best in the Cape. The 1983 is the latest available and, as usual, carries the Superior certification. It is vintage dated.
Allesverloren Shiraz ★★★★ The first release, from the 1982 vintage, is a super wine, more in the style of an Australian than a South African Shiraz. It is a big wine in every way (nose, flavour, body and alcohol – exceeding 13 per cent), so treat it with due respect. It is ageing well. There have been no releases of the 1983, 1984 and 1985, but the 1986 could be everything the 1982 is – and more.
Alto Cabernet Sauvignon ★★★★ A big, specially matured, full-bodied, deep-coloured, Cabernet. The 1984 is very good.
Fleur du Cap Pinotage ★★★★ When the Fleur du Cap wines were introduced, This was one of the poorest of the range, but it has since developed into a really fine Pinotage. Well-balanced and medium-bodied, with good fruit and fine cultivar character, it ages very well. It needs some four to five years to show its pace, but develops well up to ten years, and sometimes longer.
Heere XVII Grand Cuvée ★★★★ Launched late in 1988, this non-vintage, bottle-fermented bubbly has good character. It was made from Pinot Noir in the traditional *méthode champenoise*. Spending two years on the lees has given this wine its special quality.
J C le Roux Pinot Noir ★★★★ Made from Pinot Noir of the 1984 vintage (grown on the Alto and Meerlust estates) and fermented in the bottle, this is almost water white, but with good flavour which developed over a year or two in the bottle. The 1986 will be the next release.
La Motte Cabernet Sauvignon ★★★★ The 1985 vintage provided the first release of this fine wine, in 1990, from the revitalized Rupert-owned estate. Lightish in colour, this Cabernet has deep, concentrated, intense cultivar character, lots of nose and good

The carved, wooden maturation vats of Bergkelder line the walls of their underground cellar. The cellar is dug into the side of the Papagaaiberg, hence the name Bergkelder.

backing of new wood. The 1986 may be released in mid-1991.

La Motte Shiraz ★★★★ The 1985 provided the first release from this cellar. A lovely wine, full of individual character, it has lots of aroma and full, distinctive flavour. This Shiraz will age with great benefit.

Le Bonheur Blanc Fumé ★★★★ This fine, dry Sauvignon Blanc was introduced in 1981. The 1989 is promising considering the poor vintage.

L'Ormarins Cabernet Sauvignon ★★★★ (These wines are sold under the name 'Maison du Roi' in honour of the first owner.) The release of the 1983 L'Ormarins Cabernet was made only in 1988. It is a deep, rich wine with a lot of good wood, which will benefit with age. The 1984 is a fuller wine, deep, rich and full of tannin. It will develop well with time.

L'Ormarins Chardonnay ★★★★ The 1987 was the first release; it has good citrus character and is already showing some bottle age.

L'Ormarins Franschhoek Riesling ★★★★ A prolific gold-medal winner both regionally and nationally, this is a very well-made, big wine and one of the Cape's best representatives of the cultivar. The

lovely 1989 is not quite dry.

L'Ormarins Shiraz ★★★★ The 1983 was the first release and is a medium-bodied, lighter-type, yet full-flavoured Shiraz. It was launched late in 1988 in very small quantities, and is retailing at a very high price. The 1984 is bold, yet elegant and full of flavour, and is developing well.

Meeredal Pinotage ★★★★ This is one of the big Pinotage wines, wood-matured and with a good balance between wood and cultivar. It ages well in the bottle, showing great improvement over a few years. The 1984 and 1985 are big, attractive wines. The wine is only released after five years.

Meerlust Merlot ★★★★ The 1984 vintage was the first Merlot bottled under the Meerlust name. It is a beautiful wine with a depth of character embracing a concentration of fine Merlot fruit fragrances and flavours. Backed with good wood and touched with a small fraction of Cabernet, it is a most attractive wine to drink now, but one which will certainly develop over the next few years. There was no release from the 1985 vintage. The 1986 is bigger and better.

Stellenryck Blanc Fumé ★★★★ This

is an extrmemely good, unwooded wine which develops beautifully with two to three years of bottle ageing. It is dry, with a high natural acidity and the distinctive flavour of grassiness and gunflint typical of a wine made from Sauvignon Blanc in the Sancerre style.

Uitkyk Carlsheim ★★★★ Throughout the 1970s this was a pleasant, off-dry, Steen-based blend. In 1981, however, a considerable amount of Sauvignon Blanc was introduced, producing a delightfully dry wine. The 1988 is a big, bold wine full of cultivar character that is as enjoyable now as it was when young. It will be well worth keeping two or more years to develop its potential. The 1989 is a little more subdued.

Zandvliet Cabernet Sauvignon ★★★★ The 1984 is a surprisingly good wine and drinks very well.

Allesverloren Tinta Barocca ★★★(★)
Alto Rouge ★★★(★)
De Wetshof Chardonnay ★★★(★)
De Wetshof Edeloes ★★★(★)
De Wetshof Rhine Riesling ★★★(★)
De Wetshof Sauvignon Blanc ★★★(★)
Fleur du Cap Chardonnay ★★★(★)
Fleur du Cap Riesling ★★★(★)
Fleur du Cap Shiraz ★★★(★)

Fleur du Cap Spesiale Laatoes ★★★(★)
Goede Hoop Vintage Rouge ★★★(★)
Grünberger Blanc de Blanc ★★★(★)
Jacobsdal Pinotage ★★★(★)
J C le Roux Chardonnay ★★★(★)
Le Bonheur Chardonnay ★★★(★)
L'Ormarins Guldpfennig Guldenlese ★★★(★)
L'Ormarins Sauvignon Blanc ★★★(★)
L'Ormarins Rhine Riesling ★★★(★)
Meerendal Shiraz ★★★(★)
Meerlust Pinot Noir ★★★(★)
Middelvlei Pinotage ★★★(★)
Theuniskraal Gewürztraminer ★★★(★)
Uitkyk Shiraz ★★★(★)
Zandvliet Shiraz ★★★(★)
Fleur du Cap Premier Grand Crû ★★★
Fleur du Cap Emerald Stein ★★★
Fleur du Cap Natural Light ★★★
Grünberger Spritziger ★★★
Grünberger Stein ★★★
Heere XVII Souverein ★★★
J C le Roux La Chanson ★★★
J C le Roux Le Domaine ★★★
J C le Roux Sauvignon Blanc ★★★
Koopmanskloof Blanc de Marbonne ★★★.
Koopmanskloof Rhine Riesling ★★★
Kupferberger Auslese ★★★

L'Ormarins Pinot Gris ★★★
Rietvallei Chardonnay ★★★
Theuniskraal Riesling ★★★
Uitkyk Riesling ★★★
Hazendal Freudenlese ★★
Bonfoi Ouverture (no rating)
Goede Hoop Cabernet Sauvignon (no rating)
Hazendal Blanc Fumé (no rating)

La Motte Blanc Fumé (no rating)
La Motte Sauvignon Blanc (no rating)
Mont Blois Blanc Fumé (no rating)
Mont Blois Chardonnay (no rating)
Pongrácz (no rating)
Rietvallei Dry Rhine Riesling (no rating)

KAAPZICHT

The farm of Kaapzicht is situated up on the Bottelary Hills, overlooking the Cape Flats to Table Mountain and Cape Town. The cellar was built in 1946, and began to bottle a very small portion of its production to sell under its own label in 1984. Kaapzicht regularly bottles Weisser Riesling, either dry or as a Special Late Harvest. Very small quantities are produced.

ADDRESS: Kaapzicht Estate, P. O. Box 5, Sanlamhof 7532
TELEPHONE: (021) 903 3870
WINE SALES AND TASTING:
Weekdays: 08h00 to 18h00
Saturdays: 08h00 to 12h00

Tastings by appointment.
CELLAR TOURS: Guided cellar tours are held by appointment.
WINES:
Weisser Riesling ★★★

KANONKOP

This estate is easy to find, being just nine kilometres from Stellenbosch on the main road to Paarl (R44). The entrance is clearly marked by a large mounted canon.

One of the earliest estates to begin bottling in the modern era was Kanonkop way back in 1973. It was owned by wine man/statesman, Paul Sauer, but made famous by rugby Springbok, Jan Boland Coetzee, who set the standards and determined that the estate should be one of the Cape's producers of great red wine. Today, the property is owned by the Krige family, descendants of Oom Paul, with the wine being made by the ebullient Beyers Truter.

Besides being leaders in the quality-red-wine area, Kanonkop is also an innovator in marketing, being one of the earliest estates to introduce a futures scheme in the sale of their wines, and to use patent metal closures alongside traditional corks, allowing consumers to determine for themselves which closure produces the better wine over a period of time.

Kanonkop has always had a fine reputation for Pinotage, being one of the earliest farms to have grown this variety. This confidence in the variety was vindicated in 1987 when Beyers' Pinotage gave him the Diners Club Winemaker of the Year Award. As much as there is a place in the Cape for Bordeaux blends, there is a very definite place for Pinotages and those that Kanonkop make are a bench mark for other wine producers.

ADDRESS: Kanonkop Estate, P. O. Box 19, Muldersvlei 7606
TELEPHONE: (02231) 9 4656
WINE SALES AND TASTING:
Weekdays: 08h30 to 12h30 and 13h30 to 16h30
Saturdays: 10h00 to 13h00
Some of the wines may be tasted. Tastings are free of charge.
CELLAR TOURS: Guided cellar tours are held by appointment.
RESTAURANT: An informal 'Snoekbraai' under the oaks or in the Paul Sauer wine cellar can be arranged for groups of between 15 and 30 people. Bookings must be made three days in advance.
WINES:
Cabernet Sauvignon ★★★★★ A deep rich elegant wine of powerful character. Kanonkop has made such interesting wines for so many years that the cellar's former wine maker, 'Boland' Coetzee, was constantly challenged to maintain the consistently high quality. The Cabernets vary with the vintage but are always very good and feature

Baron von Stiernhielm, from the tiny European state of Lievland (which no longer exists) bought this farm – hence the name.

regularly at the Nederburg Auction. The 1987 is everything a Cabernet should be, with lovely fruit flavours and excellent wood.
Paul Sauer Fleur ★★★★(★) This wine was planned by Jan 'Boland' Coetzee over many years. He planted a vineyard comprising 55 per cent Cabernet Sauvignon, 25 per cent Cabernet Franc, 10 per cent Malbec and Souzão, and 10 per cent Merlot, all of which are harvested and crushed together. The 1986 is superb. The 1987 is still to be released.
Pinotage ★★★★ This has long been one of South Africa's bench-mark wines: big and bold with a lot of complex cultivar character

mingling well with good wood. The 1988 and 1989 continue in character and prove that this cellar continually makes one of the greatest Pinotage wines. They are also excellent value for money.
Pinot Noir ★★★★ The first vintage was that of 1978, and it has developed well. The last Pinot Noir to be sold as such by this cellar is the 1987, and is probably their best. The wine is being dropped from their range to enable concentration on their other reds.
Sauvignon Blanc ★★★(★)
Kadette ★★★
Weisser Riesling ★★★
Kadette Rooiwyn ★★

LIEVLAND

Almost on the Paarl side of the northwestern end of the Simonsberg is Lievland, an estate which has really come into its own as a quality producer in recent years. The owner, energetic dynamo Paul Benade, and wine maker, Abe Beukes, have developed the property and its cellar into a large producer of very good wine, with lots of local and international awards to prove their quality.

The reds have gained a great deal of attention, and deservedly so. Alphen Wine of the Month Club selected their Shiraz twice in a row, a wine which also won an award at the International Wine and Spirit Competition in 1989. Their Cabernet is very good and their Bordeaux blend should be excellent. Although their whites have not demanded the same attention as their reds, they should have, having collected even more international acclaim. In spite of the achievements of their

of things, the dogs are a hobby, and on top of it all they have a super place to live.

ADDRESS: Louisvale, P. O. Box 542, Stellenbosch 7600
TELEPHONE: (02231) 7 4022/9 9324

WINE SALES AND TASTING: Visitors by appointment only.

ROZENDAL FARM

This is not the easiest farm to find, though it is almost in Stellenbosch, with its fence forming the border with the suburb of Kronendal up Lanzerac way. Take the road up towards Jonkershoek, and the last road left as you leave the residential area is Omega. This leads directly into the Rozendal property, tucked beneath the forests of the Jonkershoek mountains. The estate is not geared for tourists but, as Kurt Ammann makes excellent red wine, it's well worth a visit to obtain a case or two made in the most simple of Cape cellars.

Kurt Ammann is a Swiss chef by training and originally made his reputation in South Africa with his famous food in restaurants such as the Brixton Tower in Johannesburg and Doornbosch in Stellenbosch. Now totally out of the restaurant business, he concentrates his talents for good taste on the making of fine, individualistic red wine.

The inventive and colourfully illustrated labels on Rozendal's annual production of magnums – either featuring artist Larry Scully's pictures of Stellenbosch, or Ammann's wife Lyn's work, or even the art of his youngest daughter – have made these bottles collector's items.

ADDRESS: Rozendal Farm.
P. O. Box 160, Stellenbosch 7600
TELEPHONE: (02231) 7 6855

WINE SALES AND TASTING: Visitors by appointment only.

RUSTENBERG

Rustenberg/Schoongezicht is not on the Stellenbosch Wine Route, but a visit to Stellenbosch's wineries not including this one would be like visiting the cathedrals of Rome and not going to St Peters. The property has a long history, dating back to 1682 when Roelof Pasman obtained a grant of land from Willem Adriaan van der Stel.

An example of the very best, Rustenberg, or as its owners affectionately refer to it, 'Schoon', is a real picture-postcard place – except that everything works, and works at its best. The beautiful setting with its Simonsberg backdrop, old, well-maintained oaks, green meadows dotted with Jersey cows from one of the country's champion herds, and probably the best-known, most-photographed Cape Dutch homestead in the Stellenbosch area make a visit extremely memorable – not to mention the fine, gentle folk who own the farm and work there. In 1992, the property will celebrate not just its tercentenary, but also 100 years of continuous bottling – which no other Cape estate can claim, not even Groot Constantia.

The farm is owned by the Barlow family and managed by Simon Barlow, with the wines being made by Etienne le Riche. Their red wines are legend, and their Chardonnay is comparable with the best.

To get there, head up through Ida's Valley, and follow the Rustenberg/Schoongezicht signs. Well before the High Rustenberg Hydro on the left you will see the gate of Schoongezicht.

top wines, their everyday drinkers are well priced and good, palate-pleasing products.

This is a good-looking property to visit, with the sales-and-tasting room well geared for visitors. The tasting area can also be hired for private functions.

ADDRESS: Lievland, P. O. Box 66, Klapmuts 7625
TELEPHONE: (02211) 5226
WINE SALES AND TASTING:
Weekdays: 09h00 to 17h00
Saturdays: 09h00 to 13h00
Tastings are free of charge.
CELLAR TOURS: Guided cellar tours are held by appointment.
WINES:

Weisser Riesling ★★★★ A well-made, off-dry wine with good cultivar character, the 1986 was tremendous and was recognized by

the Wine Olympiad in Paris. The 1989 is lighter than usual, but a delightful product. Apparently drier, it has lots of fine flavour and good spicy-citrus nose.
Cabernet Sauvignon ★★★(★)
Noble Late Harvest ★★★(★)
Rood ★★★(★)
Shiraz ★★★(★)
Bukettraube ★★★
Kerner Special Late Harvest ★★★
Lievlander ★★★
Sauvignon Blanc ★★★
Cheandrie ★★(★)

LOUISVALE

Although visits to Louisvale are by appointment only, mention is made because their Chardonnay is just so good.

In Devon Valley, a little way up the road from Clos Malverne and well signposted, is the small farm owned by Hans Froehling and Leon Stemmet, two ex-computer, ex-Johannesburg folk. They have teamed up with Neil Ellis, whose winery is on their property and who makes their wine.

Breeders of champion miniature Schnauzers, these two delightful gentlemen seem to really have the best of everything: their vineyard is totally managed by Leon (it's small enough to be given minute attention to detail and large enough to be economically viable), they have an expert to make their wine, Hans looks after the administration side

ADDRESS: Rustenberg, P. O. Box 33, Stellenbosch 7600
TELEPHONE: (02231) 7 3153
FAX: (02231) 7 8466
WINE SALES AND TASTING:
Weekdays: 08h30 to 12h30 and 14h00 to 16h30
Tastings are free of charge.

CELLAR TOURS: Guided cellar tours are held by appointment
WINES:
Blanc Fumé ★★★
Muscat de Frontignan ★★★
Rhine Riesling ★★★
Schoongezicht ★★★

STELLENBOSCH FARMERS' WINERY

The foremost South African Wine Operation has its headquarters on the southern outskirts of Stellenbosch (R310). The tourist centre is situated across the road from the impressive entrance to the winery, at the Oude Libertas complex. Here is where the winery tours begin, and where the audio-visual is shown and tastings take place.

During the summer months, the Oude Libertas amphitheatre is the venue for a variety of performances – ballet, drama, classical music, ethnic music, modern music and light entertainment. Some of the best of local and overseas artists perform at the amphitheatre. Some Sunday afternoons, popular music concerts are held where one may picnic on the lawns above the amphitheatre while listening to the music. Booking for shows is essential, watch the press for the programme of events.

ADDRESS: Stellenbosch Farmers' Winery, P. O. Box 46, Stellenbosch 7600
TELEPHONE: (02231) 7 3400
WINE SALES AND TASTING: No cellar sales.
Tastings are held on weekday afternoons and cost R5-00; or see 'Cellar tours'.

CELLAR TOURS: Guided cellar tours, including an audio-visual and a wine tasting, are held on weekday mornings at R5-00 a head (children under 18, free of charge) – booking advisable (Tel. (02231) 7 3400 ask for tour division (ext. 2473)).

THELEMA MOUNTAIN VINEYARDS

That Gyles Webb has one of the finest palates in the country should not be surprising, as Gyles is a remarkable person. He was born in Natal, and an education at Michaelhouse and Natal University presented the world with a top-notch golfer with a degree in accounting. However, he had been bitten by the wine bug, so it was off to the University of Stellenbosch to obtain a degree in oenology. From there he did time at SFW, most of which was in their experimental cellar, before taking himself off to California to work a season with the famous Joe Heitz.

Then came the life-long ambition – the vineyard and cellar of his own. In 1983 he acquired a run-down fruit farm at the top of Helshoogte on the southern slopes of the Simonsberg, and set about removing the fruit and establishing vineyards that were as near perfect as possible. When an arrangement to make use of John Platter's cellar fell through with the sale of Delaire in 1987, Gyles moved with his usual speed and had one of the most attractive and well-organized cellars in the Cape built in time for the 1988 vintage – a cellar that has a view from its tasting area that is hard to match anywhere in the world.

Gyles's speed and efficiency have also helped him achieve wines of a quality that some wine makers hardly reach in a lifetime. His Sauvignon Blanc and Blanc Fumé have been instant successes, while his Chardonnay is one of the best. Red wines take a little longer even for Gyles, but, judging from cellar samples, his Cabernet will be well worth waiting for.

The farm is open for sales and tasting during the week and on Saturdays, and you will always be assured of a friendly welcome, especially from Fred!

ADDRESS: Thelema, P. O. Box 2234, Dennesig 7601
TELEPHONE: (02231) 9 1924
WINE SALES AND TASTING:
Weekdays: 09h00 to 12h30 and 14h00 to 17h00
Saturdays: 09h00 to 13h30
Tastings are free of charge.
CELLAR TOURS: There are no cellar tours as such, but the cellars are open for people to view.
WINES:
Chardonnay ★★★★ The first release from the 1988 vintage is an elegant wine with a fine, fruity, pearlike nose and full, soft flavour backed by the fine use of good wood. It tasted good on release, but is now beginning to develop its potential. The 1989 is one of the Cape's best, and is full of the intense flavours of citrus, lime, peach and toasty wood – a lovely wine.
Sauvignon Blanc ★★★★ The first vintage was from 1987, and was remarkable for the intensity achieved from such young vines on this newish wine farm. The 1989 is a

Imposing 11 000-litre casks stand in an SFW cellar. Despite the present popularity of small wood, large vats are still much used.

super wine and the best to date, with a very good cultivar character. It is very good value for money.
Blanc Fumé ★★★(★)

Rhine Riesling ★★★(★)
Cabernet Sauvignon (no rating)
Wood-matured Dry White (no rating)

VERGENOEGD

This 300-year-old family estate (originally granted to Pieter de Vos in 1696) is the closest to False Bay of any of the Stellenbosch farms, and has the Eerste River wind its way through the property before it flows under the N2 and out to False Bay. With its magnificent Cape Dutch complex, it has held its old-world charm, and still sports magnificent old horses, although they are no longer used for the pulling of ploughs or wagons – they do look good on the pasture, though.

Young John Faure is now at the helm of wine making here, and has been responsible for replanting with varieties such as Merlot and Cabernet Franc, as well as new Cabernet Sauvignon, which, together with fresh small oak should herald a new era at Vergenoegd.

When visiting Vergenoegd keep an eye out for the geese – not that they are menacing, they are simply some of the country's top prize-winning birds.

Coming from Cape Town, turn left off the N2 onto the R103 and the very first farm on the right-hand side (less than a kilometre from the turnoff) is Vergenoegd.

ADDRESS: Vergenoegd Estate, P. O. Box 1, Faure 7131
TELEPHONE: (024) 4 3248
WINE SALES AND TASTING:
Wednesdays: 14h00 to 17h00
Any other time by appointment. There are tastings for those interested in buying. They are free of charge.
CELLAR TOURS: There are no cellar tours.

WINES:
Cabernet Sauvignon ★★★★(★) A style of wine very distinctive of the estate, and no doubt influenced by its close proximity to the sea. It is medium bodied with great depth of character, giving a very long-lasting finish and an interesting complexity. Wood-aged in old vats, it is constantly certified Superior. It develops well over five to 10 years,

The brand names of many famous wines are featured on the buildings of the Stellenbosch Farmers' Winery.

is sold regularly at the Nederburg Auction and, in earlier days, was a consistent grand champion at the South African Championship Wine Show.

Cinsaut ★★★★ A really good Cinsaut which is easy to drink at two years, and develops really well in the bottle. The 1986 was released in 1988 and is a delightful, light-bodied, well-flavoured wine that drinks very easily.

Shiraz ★★★★ First released on the open market in 1978, this attractive, deep, red wine had the character to develop well with time, peaking in about 1985/7. The 1985 has the kind of cultivar character which tends towards 'leather' as opposed to 'smoky' which is characteristic of the 1986.

Pinotage ★★★

Port ★★★

Tinta Barocca ★★★

Sauvignon Blanc ★★

WARWICK

Warwick was originally part of a larger farm founded by Colonel William Alexander Gordon and called Good Success. Some of the best wine-making grapes in the Stellenbosch area have been growing for many years on Warwick, and supplied to merchant cellars. The farming aspect is in the hands of Stan Ratcliffe – one of his many highly successful business ventures.

However, Stan's diminutive Canadian-born wife, Norma, decided that she wished to make the best wine in the Cape, and took herself off to Bordeaux to learn the trade. There, Norma's teacher broke his leg, and Norma was forced to take over the physical wine making for the vintage. She learned quickly and obviously well.

In a few short years – the first wines were bottled only in 1985 – Norma's reputation has grown. Her Trilogy, Cabernet and Merlot are all magnificent, not to mention her Cabernet Franc, which so impressed a much-respected English wine merchant that he convinced her to bottle it especially for him.

Though Norma is principly a red-wine maker, she has also begun to produce – on encouragement from her assistant, Lola Hunting – a good Chardonnay, as well as a delightful Noble Late Harvest from Sauvignon Blanc.

ADDRESS: Warwick Farm, P. O. Box 2, Muldersvlei 7606
TELEPHONE: (02231) 9 4410

WINE SALES AND TASTING: By appointment only.

ZEVENWACHT

The approach to Zevenwacht is through the town of Kuilsrivier, but the vineyards stretch out along the Bottelary Hills. The farm is owned by well-known Cape Town architect Gilbert Colyn, and its wines were put on the map by the talented Neil Ellis. Neil has left, and wine making is now in the hands of his ex-assistant, Eric Saayman.

Zevenwacht's shareholders can make use of accommodation on the farm, and there is also a restaurant for their use. Currently being developed is a 250-cottage complex, which will give owners the feel of living on a wine estate and magnificent views towards Table Bay.

ADDRESS: Zevenwacht, P. O. Box 387, Kuilsrivier 7580
TELEPHONE: (021) 903 5123
FAX: (021) 903 3373
WINE SALES AND TASTING:
Weekdays: 08h30 to 12h30 and 13h30 to 17h00
Saturdays: 09h30 to 12h30
Wine tasting costs R2-50.
CELLAR TOURS: Guided cellar tours are held by appointment.
RESTAURANT: The restaurant is reserved for the estate's shareholders.
WINES:
Gewürztraminer ★★★★ The first release from the 1986 vintage was almost dry, with good nose and full flavour. It has developed well in the bottle. The 1989 appears to be dry and has good nose and flavour.

Blended Red ★★★(★)
Rhine Riesling ★★★(★)
Blanc de Blanc ★★★
Blanc de Noir ★★★
Bouquet Blanc ★★★
Cabernet Sauvignon ★★★
Sauvignon Blanc ★★★
Special Late Harvest ★★★
Stein ★★(★)
Pinotage ★★
Rosé ★★
Shiraz ★★
Vin Blanc ★★
Zevenrood ★★
Pinot Noir (no rating)

Paarl

The town of Paarl is situated in the scenic Berg River valley, flanked by Paarl Mountain and the towering Drakenstein range. The Berg River flows through the length of the valley and the vineyards are distributed over three main types of soil. This, together with mountain slopes and a river valley, gives Paarl wines a wide range of style.

The town has an old world charm with its incredibly long main street, one end of which is dominated by the sprawling complex of the headquarters of the KWV. The town also has the oldest church still in use as a place of worship in South Africa, the Dutch Reformed 'Strooidak' (thatched-roof) church in the main street.

A landmark in the area is the Afrikaans Language Monument (Taalmonument), situated at the eastern end of the Paarl Mountain. The monument was unveiled on 12 October 1975, and commemorates a long and ultimately successful campaign to give Afrikaans equal status with English.

No account of the attractions of Paarl would be complete without mention of Wagonwheels (Tel. (02211) 2 5265). This excellent restaurant, owned and hosted by Robert and Gabi, serves what are quite simply the best steaks in the Cape, done with a variety of excellent sauces. Wagonwheels is licensed, but you may take your own wine.

An important event on the Paarl wine calendar is the Annual Paarl Nouveau Festival, to which the Paarl wine makers deliver their fresh Nouveau in all manner of unique transport. It is a fun-filled day, with food stalls, wine stalls etc. It is essential to buy your tickets in advance; they are available from the Paarl Wine Route Office (P. O. Box 46, Paarl – Tel. (02211) 2 3605).

The Paarl Wine Route is quite easy to reach from Cape Town (about an hour's drive), but if you do wish to stay in the area there are a number of different types of accommodation available. Contact your nearest tourist information bureau for further details.

BACKSBERG

Under the innovative leadership of Sydney Back, Backsberg has always been at the forefront of development in the Cape wine scene. One of the Cape's earliest wineries to register as an estate under the 1973 Wine of Origin Legislation, Backsberg has always welcomed visitors. A self-guided tour was installed very early on, and the winery also has a modest but interesting museum.

Sydney Back, besides making very good drinking wines, has proved his top-quality status by twice being the South African champion wine maker, and his 1986 Chardonnay was judged the best dry South African White Wine at the International Wine and Spirit Competition in London in 1988.

ADDRESS: Backsberg, P. O. Box 1, Klapmuts 7625
TELEPHONE: (02211) 5141/2
FAX: (02211) 5144
WINE SALES AND TASTING:
Weekdays: 08h30 to 17h30
Saturdays: 08h30 to 13h00
Wine may be tasted free of charge.
CELLAR TOURS: Visitors can go on a self-guided tour, aided by an audio-visual display and colour-coded routes.
HISTORICAL ATTRACTIONS: There is a small museum where one can see old wine-making machinery.
WINES:
Cabernet Sauvignon ★★★★(★) A light, elegant wine with a fine Cabernet character which makes remarkably good drinking at a very young age. This was the first wine to be awarded Superior status under the Wine of Origin Legislation, and is a regular prize winner. Most vintages have Superior status and are undoubtedly excellent, and all have considerable varietal character. They are surprisingly consistent wines: throughout the 1970s there was very little variation from vintage to vintage. All are ageing well, and it is hard to choose between the years.
Chardonnay ★★★★(★) The original limited releases of the 1980 and 1981 vintages were a little disappointing: they had perhaps more wood than cultivar character. The 1988 and 1989, however, seem to have settled into a fine, fruity style that is fairly distinctive of Backsberg.

Klein Babylonstoren ★★★★(★) In keeping with the Backsberg reds, the 1984 release was surprisingly easy to drink within three years of making. The 1987 is 40 per cent each of Cabernet and Merlot, and 20 per cent Cabernet Franc. Its character is far more intense.
John Martin ★★★★ A wine made from Sauvignon Blanc and named after the estate's late administrator, bottling man and even wine maker on occasion – indisputably a character and persuasive salesman. John was always against wood-aged or wood-treated white wine, and Sydney Back quirkily named this wood-fermented and further wood-aged wine after him. It appears that John had no choice but to learn to appreciate this massive, full-flavoured, complex wine. The 1988 is great, but it is

The Taalmonument, atop Paarl Rock, stands up behind wine and table-grape vineyards near Paarl.

worth waiting for three years to allow full potential to develop.

Méthode Champenoise ★★★★ Made by the *méthode champenoise*, and clearly labelled 'fermented in the bottle', this sparkling wine was launched in 1988, coinciding with Sydney Back's 50th anniversary of wine making on the property which now forms the Backsberg Estate. The 1986 has developed well in the bottle.

Noble Late Harvest ★★★★ To my knowledge, this is the only Gewürztraminer made in noble-late-harvest style. In spite of botrytis, the 1988 still had very good varietal character. It has developed beautifully and is a lovely wine.

Shiraz ★★★★ An extremely well-made wine with deep, distinctive Shiraz character, this has been a firm favourite over the years. The 1987 and 1988 are full of

flavour – they are lovely wines that are excellent value for money.

Special Late Harvest ★★★★ A luscious, full-flavoured, rich wine with the honeyed Steen taste, which is soft and smooth across the palate. This wine has always been good, and is now making the most of the more recent laws allowing higher sugars. It usually carries Superior certification. The 1989 is a blend of Steen, Muscat and Gewürztraminer.

Chenin Blanc ★★★(★)
Sauvignon Blanc ★★★(★)
Bukettraube ★★★
Dry Red ★★★
Hanepoot ★★★
Pinot Noir ★★★
Pinotage ★★★
Rhine Riesling ★★★
Rosé ★★★
Nouveau Rouge (no rating)

BOLANDSE CO-OPERATIVE

One of the biggest and best known co-ops in the area, Bolandse was formed by the combination of the Berg River and Perlse wine co-ops in 1976. It has an excellent record of achievements and awards, and makes a wide range of wines. In an endeavour to keep their wines affordable, they have introduced the very successful Bon Vino wines in 500-millilitre, screw-top, returnable bottles.

The co-op is situated at two locations, one near the Dal Josafat station off Dromedaris Street at the northwestern end of Paarl and the other just outside Paarl in the fork made by the two roads going to Windmeul and Malmesbury.

ADDRESS: Boland, P. O. Box 7007, Noorder-Paarl 7623 (Cellar 1); Boland, P. O. Box 2, Huguenot 7645 (Cellar 2)
TELEPHONE: (02211) 2 1766 (Cellar 1);
(02211) 62 6190 (Cellar 2)
FAX: (02211) 62 5379
WINE SALES AND TASTING:
Weekdays: 08h30 to 12h30 and 13h30 to 17h00
Saturdays: 09h00 to 12h00
Tasting is free of charge.
CELLAR TOURS: No cellar tours.
WINES:
Cabernet Sauvignon ★★★(★)
Pinotage ★★★(★)
Bukettraube ★★★
Cinsaut ★★★
Grand Crû ★★★
Chenin Blanc ★★(★)
Late Vintage ★★(★)
Port ★★(★)
Riesling ★★(★)
Bon Vino ★★
Hanepoot Jerepigo ★★
Sauvignon Blanc ★★
Sec Sparkling Wine ★★
Stein ★★
Vin Rouge ★★
Nouveau (no rating)

FAIRVIEW

Fairview, situated on the Suid-Agter Paarl Road between the R44 and the R101, offers a comprehensive range of wines with tremendous consumer appeal. Charles Back is the innovative wine maker on the estate, and has been a leader in the production of a Gamay Noir Nouveau. He has also produced the first commercial sulphur-dioxide-free wine for Woolworths.

The estate has a real farm flavour and character, and is famous not only for its wine but also its herd of Swiss Saanen goats (which were imported in 1981) and the variety of cheeses produced from their milk.

One of the most photographed buildings in the winelands.

The goat tower has become one of the winelands' most photographed buildings. The Backs also farm guinea fowls, pheasants, quails, chickens (and eggs), sheep and pigs, all of which add to the farmyard feel of the place.

ADDRESS: Fairview, P. O. Box 583, Suider-Paarl 7624
TELEPHONE: (02211) 63 2450
FAX: (02211) 63 2591
WINE SALES AND TASTING:
Weekdays: 08h30 to 18h00
Saturdays: 08h30 to 17h00
Tasting is free of charge.
CHEESE TASTING: Weekdays 08h30 to 18h00
Saturdays 08h30 to 17h00
Tasting is free of charge.
GOAT MILKING: The goats are milked for about two hours daily from 16h00.
WINES:
Cabernet Sauvignon ★★★★ This is a regular award winner at young wine shows. Early vintages were powerful, robust wines needing seven to 10 years to smooth out, but in the late 1970s and early 1980s the style changed. These wines are now medium-bodied and far more elegant, and drink well much earlier than previous vintages.
Reserve Cabernet ★★★★ From both the 1986 and 1987 vintages very good, deep, full-flavoured, small-wood-aged wines have been released. As good as they taste now, they will benefit from six to eight years' development.
Reserve Shiraz ★★★★ The early wines were full of flavour and heavy in character, and used to be consistent carriers of Superior certification. This cellar now produces regular class winners at

the Paarl Wine Show, but latest bottlings lack the big fullness of the earlier wines. The 1987 is soft, full-flavoured and the best of recent releases.
Brut ★★★(★)
Shiraz ★★★(★)
Special Late Harvest ★★★(★)
Blanc de Noir ★★★
Blanc Fumé ★★★
Bukettraube ★★★
Charles Gerard (White) ★★★
Chenin Blanc ★★★

Full Sweet Sémillon ★★★
Hanepoot ★★★
Pinotage ★★★
Pinot Noir ★★★
Rosé D'Une Nuit ★★★
Weisser Riesling ★★★
Paarl Vintage Red ★★(★)
Charles Gerard (Red) ★★
Charles Gerard Reserve ★★
Sauvignon Blanc ★★
Sweet Red ★★
Gamay Noir (no rating)

KWV

The full name for the KWV is Ko-operatiewe Wijnbouwers Vereeniging van Zuid-Afrika Beperkt, hence the fact that it is generally referred to as the KWV. The body was established by statute on 8 January 1918 (with Charles Kohler as its founding chairman), in an effort to control the serious overproduction problems of the day. The main objective, as set out in the constitution, is 'to direct, control and regulate the sale and dispersal by its members of their produce, being that of the grape, as shall secure or tend to secure for them a continuously adequate return for such produce'.

To make wine, or to grow grapes for the making of wine, in South Africa you must be a member of the KWV. Furthermore, the KWV determines growing quotas to regulate the amount of grapes grown for

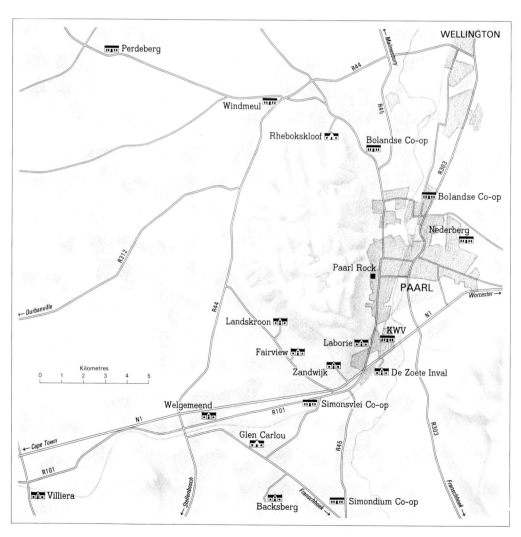

wine making. These controls give the KWV total power to determine the annual minimum to be paid for the wine produced. It is their duty to dispose of the amount of wine produced in excess to the country's consumption, which they do very efficiently – at one time mainly by exporting high-quality potable spirit and unmatured brandy. Nowadays, vast volumes (ship tankers full) of very bland wines are exported mainly to what were the Iron Curtain countries.

The KWV's colossal cellars at La Concorde are among the largest storage cellars in the world, having a total storage capacity of 2 300 000 hectolitres and boasting five of the world's largest oak vats. The cathedral cellars are to lend their name to KWV's new improved-quality range of wine for export.

ADDRESS: KWV, P. O. Box 528, Suider-Paarl 7624
TELEPHONE: (02211) 63 1001
FAX: (02211) 63 3440
WINE SALES AND TASTING: KWV wines are for export only, so wines may not be purchased. Wines may be tasted however – for wine-tasting, see 'Cellar tours'.
CELLAR TOURS: Tours of the cellars start from Kohler Street, and include a very good audio-visual presentation, a walk through the great cathedral, sherry and export cellars, and wine tasting. They are conducted in either English or Afrikaans.
Mondays, Wednesdays and Fridays: 09h30 and 14h15 (Afrikaans); 11h00 and 15h45 (English)
Tuesdays and Thursdays: 11h00 and 15h45 (Afrikaans); 09h30 and 14h15 (English)

Laborie is home to a popular restaurant for residents of, and visitors to, Paarl.

LABORIE

This estate, which lies on the slopes of the Paarl Mountain was purchased by the KWV in 1979. The entire estate – vineyards and buildings – has been completely restored, and a new wine cellar and tasting and lecture rooms have been constructed. The manor house is closed to the public, but not so the wine house and restaurant.

The modern cellar produces wines under the labels Laborie and Taillefert (Jean Taillefert was the original owner of Laborie).

ADDRESS: Laborie, P. O. Box 632, Suider-Paarl 7624
TELEPHONE: (02211) 63 2034
WINE SALES AND TASTING: Laborie wines may be bought at the off-sales, which also sells selected wines from the Paarl District.
Sales Weekdays: 09h00 to 17h00
Saturdays: 09h00 to 13h00
There is no wine tasting.
CELLAR TOURS: There are no cellar tours.
RESTAURANT: The Laborie restaurant serves à la carte dishes, as well as a buffet of traditional dishes (R20-80 plus tax) for lunch every day from 12h30 to 14h00. From Tuesdays to Saturdays, à la carte dishes are served for dinner (19h30 to 21h00). There is a set menu on Sundays (R25-00 plus tax).
WINES:
Taillefert White ★★★(★)
Blended Red ★★★
Blended White ★★★
Taillefert ★★★
Sparkling Blanc de Noir ★★★

LANDSKROON

On the WR3 is the De Villiers family's Landskroon Estate, overlooking the Joostenbergvlakte with a view to Table Mountain. The estate has been owned by the De Villiers's for over 300 years, and is home not only to vineyards, but also to a prize-winning Jersey herd from which choice cheese is made.

ADDRESS: Landskroon, P. O. Box 519, Suider-Paarl 7624
TELEPHONE: (02211) 63 1039/59
FAX: (02211) 63 2810
WINE SALES AND TASTING:
Weekdays: 08h30 to 17h30
Saturdays: 08h30 to 12h30
Tasting is free of charge.
CELLAR TOURS: There are no organized cellar tours, but visitors may wander through the cellars.
RESTAURANT: A vintner's platter is served from the middle of November to the end of April, Mondays to Fridays, between 11h30 and 14h30 at R15-26 per head.
CHEESE TASTING:
Weekdays 08h30 to 17h30
Saturdays 08h30 to 12h30
Tasting is free of charge.
WINES:
Cabernet Sauvignon ★★★★ This Cabernet has good varietal character with a rather unusual minty nose and good wood. A fair amount of bottle age is needed before it settles down. The 1988 is the best ever but will need time to develop.
Cinsaut ★★★★ A fairly fruity wine with medium body and finesse lacking in many lesser Cinsauts. It provides enjoyable drinking, proving that this cultivar, when correctly handled, can produce good dry reds.
Port ★★★★ A regular medal and trophy winner at regional and national shows, this distinctive wine was, in its earlier vintages, made from Tinta Barocca, Cinsaut and Alicante Bouschet. It is not as sweet as most local Ports, and is a little more chewy. It is vintage-dated. The 1988 has dropped Cinsaut from the blend and is in a dumpy Port bottle with one of those labels you think you have seen somewhere before. It is a good wine that will develop well.
Shiraz ★★★★ An award-winning wine with more character than most Cape Shiraz wines. Although easy to drink when young, it will develop and soften considerably in the bottle. The 1988 is full of flavour and, as drinkable as it is now, it will benefit from five to six years in the bottle. It is remarkable value for money.
Bouquet Rouge ★★★(★)
Cabernet Franc ★★★
Pinotage ★★★
Special Late Harvest ★★★
Tinta Barocca ★★★
Bouquet Blanc ★★(★)
Pinot Noir ★★(★)
Blanc de Noir ★★
Chenin Blanc ★★
Sauvignon Blanc ★★
Nouveau Rouge (no rating)

NEDERBURG

South Africa's internationally famous wine cellar has its vineyards situated along the slopes of the Drakenstein mountains and its cellar complex on the WR4, which connects the N1 (from the entrance to the Du Toits Kloof toll road) to the Dal Josafat part of Paarl.

The complex contains the Johan Graue Building – the venue for the famous annual Nederburg Auction – and the old homestead. The Nederburg Auction is the premier event on the South African wine calendar, and is an auction of rare Cape wines which has been held annually since 1975. It has developed into an international event, with major local and overseas buyers bidding for the finest wines produced by the Cape's top estates, wineries, co-ops and wholesalers .

Since their introduction in 1952, Nederburg wines have become household names, and trusted for their quality and consistency. They have won more local and international awards than any other South African wines. In 1992, Nederburg will celebrate its 200th Anniversary, and a series of events are being planned to mark the occasion.

ADDRESS: Nederburg, P. O. Box 46, Huguenot 7645
TELEPHONE: (02211) 62 3104
FAX: (02211) 62 4887
WINE SALES AND TASTING:
Sales Weekdays: 08h30 to 17h00
For tastings see 'Cellar tours'.
CELLAR TOURS: Cellar tours – which include an audio-visual display and wine tasting – take place Mondays to Fridays by appointment. They are conducted regularly in Afrikaans and English and on request in French and German.
WINES:
Gewürztraminer ★★★★★
Nederburg Gewürztraminer was originally sold at the annual Auction as a delicate, semi-sweet white with true rose-petal nose. More recently it has been released as a 'special'. Twice in succession it has been awarded the trophy for best Gewürztraminer on show at the Club Oenologique International Wine and Spirit competition. This wine has outstanding nose with full, rich flavour enhanced by the excellent sugar acid balance.
Edelrood ★★★★(★) Edelrood is a top-quality dry red in which no particular variety shows, but as a harmonious whole it is hard to beat. Originally it was launched as an uncomplicated, pleasant, dry table wine of light body and acid with moderate tannin, recent vintages have taken on a more definite and demanding style: it is now a wine to be reckoned with and one that needs time to show its best. Edelrood ages extremely well and is destined to be the best of Nederburg's – and therefore one of the best of South Africa's – red wines
Paarl Cabernet Sauvignon ★★★★(★) The Cabernets of Nederburg are internationally renowned for their own distinctive style of deep,red richness in which cultivar character is heavily prominent. Delicious and full, they require good bottle ageing before they reach their full potential (they peak between 10 and 15 years). Attractive as they are when young, they should not really be opened before they are at least five years old and are beginning to show some of their promise. Patience and self-denial will be amply rewarded. Nederburg elevated Cabernet to the most sought-after cultivar in South Africa.
Baronne ★★★★ The first four vintages of Baronne – 1973, 1974, 1975, 1976, – varied considerably but were all excellent wines and have matured magnificently. A very definite style of wine has now emerged, not far removed from the Nederberg Selected Cabernets of old, which were reputed to be blends containing predominantly Cabernet and lesser quantities of Shiraz, Pinotage and Cinsaut. Whatever the composition, the result is fine, full-flavoured, deep-red wine which is acceptably good when young but has every potential for fine ageing. This wine has a very good berry-like aroma and flavour, and will bring true delight if aged for five years or more.
Cabernet Sauvignon Blanc de Noir ★★★★ Initially produced from the 1982 vintage, this was the first Blanc de Noir to carry a cultivar claim and to achieve Superior certification. Each subsequent vintage has been dry, elegant and gentle yet persistent with a most attractive aroma and a light but fine flavour. Best when young.
Kap Sekt ★★★★ Produced originally for export to Germany where, to qualify for the appellation 'Sekt', this wine had to be aged for at least one year. Each vintage has carried Superior certification.
Pinot Noir ★★★★ The first release of this limited edition was from the 1982 vintage. A firm fine wine with clear cultivar character and reserved use of new oak, it is of high quality and certainly good value for money.
Prelude ★★★★ The first release from the 1988 vintage appeared early in 1990, the launch coinciding with the 16th Nederberg Auction. It is a very good blend of Sauvignon Blanc and Chardonnay that has been just sufficiently wood-aged to tone the components but not to be obviously woody. A wine with plenty of potential to develop well in the bottle, it nevertheless makes very good drinking now.
Rhine Riesling ★★★★ A welcome addition (in 1981) to this cellar's range, this wine has been tremendously successful in terms of public acceptance, awards and Superior certification. An off-dry, well-flavoured wine with good cultivar character, it has enough acid to be attractive when young, yet is able to age with benefit.
Special Late Harvest ★★★★ South Africa's leading late harvest wine which has enjoyed many, many years of acclaim for its high quality. This Wine of Origin Paarl is full of sweet richness, genuinely developed from grapes allowed to age on the vine prior to pressing. In recent years it has had very good botrytis, or noble rot, character which puts it in a class of its own. With the most recent definitions of sweetness legally classifying late harvest wines, the Nederburg is automatically classed as Special Late Harvest and is always certified Superior. When allowed to age for three or four years, a luscious wine of intense depth develops, an outstanding example of an elegant

The famous Cape Flemish homestead at Nederburg was built in 1800 by German immigrant Philip Wolvaart.

Rhebokskloof is a relative newcomer to the Cape winelands, but no expense is being spared to restore the estate.

Cinsaut ★★(★)	Riesling ★★
Colombar ★★(★)	Chenin Blanc Semi-Sweet (no
Cinsaut Liqueur Wine ★★	rating)
Late Vintage ★★	Muscat d'Alexandrie (no rating)

RHEBOKSKLOOF

One of the Paarl Wine Route's finest showpieces, this newcomer to the route has been lovingly restored. Consisting of a number of farms that have been consolidated to form one estate, this is a rare venture in that there is a table grape operation alongside vineyards growing grapes for wine. The estate also rears sheep, which not only add to the picturesque setting, but also supply super lamb for the restaurant.

A pair of black eagles have made their home on Rhebokskloof – which borders the Paarl Mountain Nature Reserve – and they can often be seen circling high above the estate.

ADDRESS: Rhebokskloof, P. O. Box 2125, Windmeul 7630
TELEPHONE: (02211) 63 8386
FAX: (02211) 63 8504
WINE SALES AND TASTING:
Sales Daily: 09h00 to 17h00
Tastings take place Mondays to Sundays (weekdays: 09h00 to 17h30, weekends: 10h00 to 16h00). They are free of charge. Large groups are welcome by appointment.
CELLAR TOURS: Cellar tours are held by appointment.
RESTAURANT: The traditional Cape Restaurant is open seven days a week for lunch (12h00 to 14h30): on weekdays and Sundays, a buffet lunch is served (weekdays R35-00, Sundays R38-00) and on Mondays to Saturdays light terrace lunches (minimum charge R15-00) can be obtained. The Victorian dining room is open for à la carte lunches Mondays to Fridays and dinners Wednesdays, Fridays and Saturdays (19h00 to 00h00). Booking is essential. This is one of the few places that one can get morning and afternoon tea (09h30 to 12h00 and 15h00 to 17h00). For all restaurant bookings, phone (02211) 63 8606.
TOURS: The estate offers a 35-minute tour of the vineyards in an open four-wheel-drive, weather permitting, that includes some magnificent views across the Cape Flats to Table Mountain and the Atlantic Ocean. Bookings advisable.
WINES:
Cabernet Sauvignon ★★★(★)
Blanc Fumé ★★★
Bouquet Blanc ★★★
Première Cuvée ★★★
Special Late Harvest ★★★
St Felix Vineyards Tamay Sparkling Wine ★★★
Grand Vin Blanc ★★(★)
Nouveau (no rating)

and gentle botrytis wine. Eight successive vintages have carried Superior certification.
Première Cuvée Brut ★★★(★)
Première Cuvée Doux ★★★(★)
Premier Grand Crû ★★★(★)
Stein ★★★(★)
Elegance ★★★
Nouvelle Light ★★★
Paarl Riesling ★★★
Rosé ★★★
Rosé Sec ★★★
Gamay Noir (no rating)

PAARL ROCK

Although part of the Paarl Wine Route, this cellar makes brandy rather than wine. Situated on Dromedaris Street, this quaint, almost museum-like operation is the only brandy distillery and cellar where one can see the complete production of brandy from distillation through ageing to bottling. Producers of Paarl Brandy, they make visitors very welcome.

ADDRESS: Paarl Rock Brandy Cellar, P. O. Box 63, Huguenot 7645
TELEPHONE: (02211) 62 6159
CELLAR TOURS: These are conducted Monday to Friday from 11h00 to 15h00

PERDEBERG

Perdeberg's original cellar received its first grapes in the vintage of 1942. Joseph Huskisson became wine maker in 1956 and, although most of what he makes is sold in bulk to major merchants, a small amount is bottled annually. It is advisable to phone to establish if stock is available for sale at the cellar. The dry Chenin Blanc makes a visit to Perdeberg worthwhile.

ADDRESS: Perdeberg, P. O. Box 214, Paarl 7620
TELEPHONE: (02211) 63 8244/8112
FAX: (02211) 63 8245
WINE SALES AND TASTING:
Weekdays: 08h00 to 12h30 and 14h00 to 17h00
Tastings are free of charge.
CELLAR TOURS: Cellar tours are conducted by appointment Mondays to Fridays.
WINES:
Chenin Blanc ★★★
Paarl Pinotage ★★★

SIMONDIUM CO-OPERATIVE

This is the oldest co-op in the area, having been founded in 1906. The attractive many-gabled facade of the old building is unique. The co-op has suffered mixed fortunes in recent times, and was liquidated in 1990. It was then purchased by local farmer Mr Barney Marais, who intends to restore the cellar to its 'former glory'.

ADDRESS: Simondium Co-op, P. O. Box 19, Simondium 7670
TELEPHONE: (02211) 4 1659
WINE SALES AND TASTING: No sales at present.

SIMONSVLEI CO-OPERATIVE

Established in 1945 (originally with Oom Sarel Rossouw as wine maker), this co-op – on the R101 alongside the N1 – is difficult to miss, with the giant wine bottle that stands in front of the winery's cellar dominating the scene. The grapes for the co-op come from as far afield as Wemmershoek and Klein Drakenstein, and along the Berg River as far as the Simonsberg, Paarl Mountain and the gravel soils of

The huge wine bottle outside the front of Simonsvlei has proved to be a highly successful advertising gimmick. The co-operative is now one of the most-visited wineries in the region.

Muldersvlei. The variation of soil and climate allows Simonsvlei to create a full range of attractive wines, including a bubbly. The co-op boasts a long string of awards to underline its success. It specializes in producing wines with personalized labels to commemorate any special occasion.

ADDRESS: Simonsvlei, P. O. Box 584, Suider-Paarl 7624
TELEPHONE: (02211) 63 3040
FAX: (02211) 63 1240
WINE SALES AND TASTING:
Weekdays: 08h30 to 17h00
Saturdays: 08h30 to 12h30
Tastings are free of charge.
CELLAR TOURS: Guided cellar tours are available on request.
RESTAURANT: During December, light lunches (what these comprise varies from year to year) are served between 11h00 and 15h00.
WINES:
Noble Late Harvest ★★★★ This was made from Bukettraube during the 1989 vintage, and is one of the cellar's best ever wines. It is full of fruit, spice and sweetness, and is well balanced with good acid.
Pinotage ★★★★ This full- rather than medium-bodied wine is not heavy, yet it has powerful Pinotage character. Most of the grapes originate from the hot northwestern slopes of the Simonsberg, and so develop a high sugar and alcohol content – more than 13,5 per cent by volume. The wine is wood-aged for 18 months before bottling, thereafter developing well to give,

at some five or six years of age, a fully rounded and smooth wine. It is a regular award-winner at regional and national shows. Recent vintages are fine, firm wines with good fruit and ageing potential.
Muscadel Jerepigo ★★★(★)
Shiraz ★★★(★)
Cabernet Sauvignon ★★★
Chenin Blanc ★★★
Dry Steen ★★★
Hanepoot ★★★
Humbro ★★★
Port ★★★
Rhine Riesling ★★★
Sauvignon Blanc ★★★
Grand Crû ★★(★)
Riesling ★★(★)
Simonsrood ★★(★)
Special Late Harvest ★★(★)
Blanc de Blanc ★★
Blanc de Noir ★★
Bukettraube ★★
Chardonnay ★★
Late Vintage ★★
Rosé ★★
Stein ★★
Nouvcau (no rating)
Red Muscadel (no rating)
White Muscadel (no rating)

VILLIERA

At the corner of the R101 and the R304, just off the N1's Exit 15, stand the apparently humble premises of Villiera. Looks can be deceiving, however, as, behind the friendly – though somewhat casual – appearance, is one of the Cape's most magical operations.

Jeff Grier is the wine maker here, while cousin Simon grows the grapes. Though probably best known for their excellent bubblies made by the *méthode champenoise*, in conjunction with Jean Louis Denois of French-champagne origin, they also produce some outstanding white wines and tremendous reds including a magnificent Merlot. Villiera has a reputation for selling their wines at excellent value for quality – in fact, at most attractive prices.

For those with an interest in wine and the wine industry, the estate holds its St Vincent's Day Festival on 22 January yearly. Presentations and speeches are made, and these are followed by a three-course supper (wine included) for R30-00.

ADDRESS: Villiera Wine Estate, P. O. Box 66, Koelenhof 7605
TELEPHONE: (02231) 9 2002/3
FAX: (02231) 9 2314
WINE SALES AND TASTING:
Weekdays: 08h30 to 17h00
Saturdays: 08h30 to 13h00
Tastings are free of charge. The Tradition wines are not available for tasting, though they may be bought.
CELLAR TOURS: A tour of the Tradition cellar is available by appointment for groups of up to 10. The cost of the tour is R12-00 a head (essentially the price of the bottle of Tradition you receive at the end).
RESTAURANT: The estate restaurant serves light terrace lunches on weekdays from November to April between 12h00 and 14h00

(R12-00). Champagne breakfasts are served from time to time – phone the estate to find out when the next one is planned.
WINES:
Tradition de Charles de Fère Reserve ★★★★(★) Some 50 cases are sold at each of the annual Cape Independent Winemakers' Guild Auctions. The wine is never less than three years on its lees and is degorged shortly before the auction. This is a delicious bubbly that improves with each release as the cellar perfects its techniques and introduces more of the classic varieties for the blend. It is a bubbly well worth seeking out.
Estate Crû Monro ★★★★
Traditionally, Monro is the middle name of the Grier family, and it has been given to the red and white

The entrance to Villiera shows the way to the most popular méthode champenoise *cellar in the Cape.*

flagship wines of the estate. The 1986, a blend of 60 per cent Cabernet and 40 per cent Merlot, is the best release to date.

Rhine Riesling ★★★★ This wine has improved over the years: the later vintages are delightfully dry, full and fragrant. The 1988 and 1989 are finished dry, and the latter is a superb wine that will develop with distinction. The cellar is firmly established as one of the most consistent producers of fine wines from this cultivar.

Tradition de Charles de Fère ★★★★ An unusual partnership – between Villiera Estate and the Frenchman, Jean Louis Denois – led to the creation of this sparkling wine. Both red and white grapes were used in its production, the result of which is a splendid wine which is improving all the time. Excellent value for money, it is constantly one of South Africa's better *méthode champenoise* wines. In keeping with the traditions of Champagne, this cellar's main production is not vintage dated. This consistently good wine is one of my favourites.

Cabernet Sauvignon ★★★(★)
Gavotte ★★★(★)
Tradition Rosé ★★★(★)
Garonne Special Late Harvest ★★★
Operette ★★★
Sauvignon Blanc ★★★
Sonnet ★★★
Crû Monro Blanc Fumé (no rating)
Private Reserve (no rating)
Tradition Prestige Cuvée (no rating)

WINDMEUL

Very small quantities of this cellar's wines are bottled, but what there is can be bought at the cellar.

ADDRESS: Windmeul, P. O. Box 2013, Windmeul 7630
TELEPHONE: (02211) 63 8043
WINE SALES AND TASTING: Weekdays: 08h30 to 12h30 and 13h30 to 17h00
Wines may not be tasted.
CELLAR TOURS: No cellar tours are held.

ZANDWIJK

On the slopes of Paarl Mountain, is South Africa's only kosher winery, where wine making is strictly according to religious requirements. Approach the winery from Pieter Hugo Street, Suider-Paarl.

ADDRESS: Zandwijk, P. O. Box 2674, Paarl 7620
TELEPHONE: (02211) 63 2368
FAX: (02211) 63 1884
WINE SALES AND TASTING: Weekdays: 08h30 to 12h30 and 13h30 to 17h00
Tastings are free of charge.

CELLAR TOURS: Cellar tours are held by appointment only.
WINES:
Chardonnay ★★★
Klein Draken ★★(★)
Sauvignon Blanc ★★
Weisser Riesling ★★
Cabernet Sauvignon (no rating)

The following wineries are not part of the official Paarl Wine Route, but are open to the public (albeit sometimes only by appointment).

DE ZOETE INVAL

This estate is difficult to find, and so prefers to sell by fax or phone. If you are planning to buy off the farm, phone in advance to make an appointment and to get directions!

ADDRESS: De Zoete Inval Estate, P. O. Box 591, Suider-Paarl 7624
TELEPHONE: (02211) 63 2375
FAX: (02211) 63 2817
WINE SALES AND TASTING: Visitors are welcome by appointment.

GLEN CARLOU

Owned by Blaauwklippen's former wine maker (he worked there for 15 years and was responsible for that cellar's reputation for good wine), Walter Finlayson, this new venture straddles the road that connects Klapmuts to Simondium. A most attractive modern winery building sits atop a ridge and has a splendid view of the Paarl valley, Paarl Mountain and the Afrikaans Taal Monument.

Finlayson's Chardonnay cellar simply comprises two rather old, though very heavily insulated, railway containers, but the underground barrel cellar for red wines has been beautifully constructed. Producing excellent wines and specializing in Chardonnay and Merlot, Walter is not a member of the wine route, but visits to purchase can be made by appointment.

ADDRESS: Glen Carlou, P. O. Box 23, Klapmuts 7625
TELEPHONE: (02211) 5528
WINE SALES AND TASTING: Visits can be made by appointment.

WELGEMEEND

This is a tiny estate with a large reputation, owned by ex land surveyor, Billy Hofmeyer, and wife, Ursula. They make lovely, unusual and very well-priced red wines.

The estate, which was bought by the Hofmeyers in 1974 (and at the time called Monte Video), is situated on the old national road just beyond the Klapmuts junction, en route to Paarl, on the left before you reach Soopieshoogte.

ADDRESS: Welgemeend Estate, P. O. Box 69, Klapmuts 7625
TELEPHONE: (02211) 5210
WINE SALES AND TASTING: Saturdays: 09h00 to 12h30
Tastings are free of charge.
CELLAR TOURS: Guided tours of the tiny cellar are held on request.
WINES:
Blended Red ★★★★★ A multiple blend, dominated by Cabernet Sauvignon, with Cabernet Franc, Merlot, Petit Verdot and Malbec playing lesser roles. From the 1986 vintage onwards, the Malbec was dropped from the blend. The 1987 is half Cabernet Sauvignon, some 24 per cent Cabernet Franc, and Merlot making up the rest with a fraction of Petit Verdot. The result is a deep, full-flavoured wine with great character backed by good wood. The 1988 is much the same blend, although the 1987 does not have quite the same depth.
Cabernet Sauvignon ★★★★ The 1986 was the last vintage, though this wine will be reintroduced in the future. If you've got any Welgemeend wines, be selfish and drink them yourself.
Douelle ★★★★ An intriguing blend of Cabernet Sauvignon and Malbec, which develops well in the bottle. The 1987 is the best yet. The 1988 has a good range of flavours but is not quite up to the 1987.
Amadé ★★★(★)

Franschhoek

A *hoek* (corner) in the Drakenstein Mountains forms the famous Franschhoek valley. Considerable variation of soil and climatic conditions through the valley, as well as the geographical location of the vineyards – some are high on the slopes, others nestle close to the river side – have resulted in a tremendous diversity of wines from this region.

Franschhoek has been synonymous with wine production since the Huguenots settled here more than 300 years ago. (A memorial to these French refugees – possibly the best-known landmark of the region – can be seen on the T-junction at the head of Huguenot Road.) Despite its long history, however, the Franschhoek region suffered a quality decline in the post Second World War years. This has been dramatically corrected, though, and today some excellent red, white and sparkling wines are made in the valley. This re-emergence of Franschhoek as a wine area of note has been mainly due to the group of wine growers who developed the Vignerons de Franschhoek back in 1984 to promote the region's fine wines.

Although not officially part of the Vignerons de Franschhoek the 1688 Wine House in Franschhoek is a popular place for lovers of the valley's wines – tastings can be arranged by appointment. On the same premises is the well-known Le Quartier Français, a restaurant that serves a mixture of French provincial and classic Cape dishes which are honest, uncomplicated and very good – not to mention reasonably priced. The restaurant is open for lunch (12h30 to 14h00) daily, and for dinner (19h30 to 21h00) daily from October to April and on Fridays and Saturdays for the rest of the year. It is licensed, and has a wine list which naturally features wines of the area. Also on the premises is Le Cafe Français, which is open for tea, snacks and light lunches daily between 10h00 and 17h00 from October to April and Wednesdays to Sundays between 11h00 and 17h00 for the rest of the year. The telephone numbers for all of the above are (02212) 2034, 2248, 3113.

Another popular restaurant of the Franschhoek region is La Petite Ferme on the Franschhoek Pass (Tel. (02212) 3016). It boasts a magnificent view of the valley, and a menu to suit all tastes. La Petite Ferme is famous for its smoked trout – fished from the Berg River – and its fantastic puddings. The restaurant is open daily for teas and lunch (10h30 to 16h30), except for a short period during winter when it closes, and has a good list of local cellar wines, which are available at reasonable prices. Booking is essential.

If you are looking for somewhere to stay in the Franschhoek valley, you can't do better than the Swiss Farm Excelsior, a hotel which dates back to 1875. There are other accommodation options, though (including accommodation on local farms), so contact your local tourist information bureau for further information.

BELLINGHAM

Bellingham is one of South Africa's best-known wine brands. The original farm was granted to Gerrit Jansz van Vuuren in 1693, and the estate was expanded in the late 19th century, but by the 1930s it had declined to a near derelict condition. It was then purchased by Bernard Podlashuk in 1943. A marketing genius, Podlashuk rebuilt the farm, and developed the Bellingham brand, with its distinctively shaped flask. Since 1970, the farm has been owned by the Union Wine Company, which still uses the Bellingham label.

The cellar complex houses a visitors' reception area, and the estate also boasts a small amphitheatre and its very own railway siding.

ADDRESS: Bellingham Estates (Pty) Limited, P. O. Box 134, Franschhoek 7690
TELEPHONE: (02211) 4 1258
WINE SALES AND TASTING: The estate is open for sales and tasting between the beginning of December and the end of April at the following times:
Weekdays: 08h30 to 16h30
Saturdays: 10h30 to 12h00
During the remaining months, tastings are only held by appointment for groups of more than 10. Tasting is free of charge.
CELLAR TOURS: There are no cellar tours.
WINES:
Cabernet Sauvignon ★★★★(★) The first release of this wine was in 1980, and it heralded a dramatic change in the quality of Bellingham products. The 1982 is a good full wine with lots of potential. The

The Huguenot Memorial is a landmark in Franschhoek. The three arches represent the Holy Trinity, and the woman with the globe at her feet symbolizes freedom of conscience.

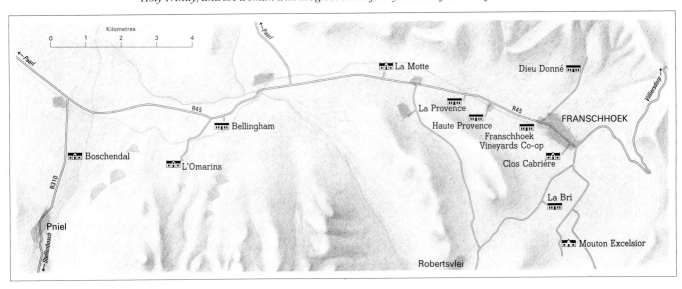

The wines of Bellingham have become household names in recent years.

Bellingham product, today's wines are rich, deep and complex, with plenty of Shiraz character. The 1985 has the smoky character so often referred to in a Shiraz yet seldom experienced. This wine regularly carries Superior certification.

Johannisberger ★★★(★)
Premier Grand Crû ★★★(★)
Special Late Harvest ★★★(★)
Almeida Rosé ★★★
Blanc de Noir ★★★
Blanc de Noir Sparkling Wine ★★★

Brut ★★★
Chardonnay ★★★
Classic Thirteen ★★★
Grande Trinité ★★★
Paarl Riesling ★★★
Pinotage ★★★
Rhine Riesling ★★★
Rosé Sec ★★★
Premier Light ★★(★)
Stein ★★(★)
Blanc de Blanc ★★
Blancenberger (no rating)

1983 is a little lighter, and probably at its best now. The 1984 and 1985 are similar in that they are much more forward wines.
Noble Late Harvest ★★★★ The first of Bellingham's limited release is a 1987 Noble Late Harvest. It is a lovely botrytised wine with good raisin character. It has developed beautifully with time.
Shiraz ★★★★ A far cry from the original no-star, non-vintage

BOSCHENDAL

Set in magnificent surroundings, Boschendal is owned by Anglo-American Farms, and they have spared nothing in giving this large estate a new lease on life, making it one of the best in the country. The vineyards are magnificently managed, and the large quantities of wine well made. Boschendal was the first winery to commercially market a Blanc de Noir in South Africa, and in so doing started a whole new market segment.

The manor house has been beautifully restored by architect Gabriel Fagan, and along with its neighbouring restaurant – which has become famous for its fare – is the centre of attraction for visitors. The Taphuis is one of the oldest buildings on the estate, and serves as tasting room and wine sales area.

The Boschendal manor house was completed in 1812, built by the then owner Paul de Villiers, for his wife, Anna Louw.

Le Pique Nique is a popular alternative to the restaurant for those wishing to have lunch at Boschendal. The gardens of the estate provide a lovely setting in which to relax.

ADDRESS: Boschendal, P. O. Box Groot Drakenstein 7680
TELEPHONE: (02211) 4 1031/4
WINE SALES AND TASTING:
Weekdays: 08h30 to 16h30
Saturdays: 08h30 to 12h30
Tastings are free of charge.
CELLAR TOURS: Although there are no cellar tours, an audio-visual presentation is held in the Ronnie van Rooyen cellar hourly from 10h30.
RESTAURANT: The restaurant serves a buffet lunch (R45-00) specializing in Cape Huguenot cuisine from 12h30 daily. From November to April, Boschendal holds Le Pique Nique (R22-50), a picnic of terrines, cold meats, salads and cheeses which you can enjoy with their wine 'al fresco' under the tall stone pines.

Booking for both the restaurant and Le Pique Nique is essential.
TOURS: Vineyard tours are held on weekdays at 11h00 and 15h00.
WINES:
Brut ★★★★ The first release of this decidedly dry wine was made from the 1979 vintage by the classic *méthode champenoise*. It was basically a Riesling, but had a good, bottle-aged character and incredibly lively, fine bubbles which gave an excellent nose. The 1986 is probably the best to date.
Brut Rosé ★★★★ The first release from the 1986 vintage is a delightful bubbly that can rank with the best. It was degorged in January 1989, and this long period on the lees has resulted in a wine with good body, lovely bouquet and fine flavour. The fresh coral-pink colour comes

from the high proportion of Pinot Noir that has been blended with mature Chardonnay grapes to form the *cuvée*. Champagne is only vintage-dated in outstanding years, and then only a portion of the production, as will be the case with Boschendal Brut Rosé.
Chardonnay ★★★★ Released in July 1989, the first wine was from the 1986 vintage. It has been disappointing and has not developed well. However, subsequent vintages have been a great improvement. The 1988 and 1989, in particular, are showing much better character.
Pinot Noir ★★★★ The first release, from the 1987 vintage, has a blackberry nose, but very little of it.

It is nice enough to drink, but, hopefully, succeeding vintages will be more attractive.
Blanc de Noir ★★★(★)
Cabernet Sauvignon ★★★(★)
Grand Vin ★★★(★)
Grand Vin Blanc ★★★(★)
Lanoy ★★★(★)
Le Bouquet ★★★(★)
Sauvignon Blanc ★★★(★)
Shiraz ★★★(★)
Blanc de Blanc ★★★
Chenin Blanc ★★★
Jean Garde Vineyard Gewürztraminer ★★★
Le Mirador ★★★
Rachelsfontein Rhine Riesling ★★★
Riesling ★★★
'Ronnie van Rooyen' Vintage Sherry ★★

The Franschhoek Valley has, historically, had a long association with wine.

CLOS CABRIÈRE

Very close to the centre of the Franschhoek village, this property specializes in *méthode champenoise* wines under the Pierre Jourdan label. The eccentric wine maker and part owner, Achim von Arnim, is also producing a farm brandy, which, due to the ageing required, will take many years to become available.

ADDRESS: Clos Cabrière Estate, P. O. Box 245, Franschhoek 7690
TELEPHONE: (02212) 2630

WINE SALES AND TASTING: No sales or tasting – visitors by appointment only.

DIEU DONNÉ

Owned by the colourful, Natal-based businessman, Robert Maingard, Dieu Donné makes its own wine, which is unusual for the Franschhoek region – many of the wines for the smaller growers are made at the local co-op.

ADDRESS: Dieu Donné Vineyards, P. O. Box 94, Franschhoek 7690
TELEPHONE: (02212) 2493
WINE SALES AND TASTING: Weekdays: 09h00 to 13h00 and 14h00 to 16h00
From mid-December to mid-January tastings are also held on Saturdays from 09h00 to 12h00.

Tastings cost R2-00 a head.
CELLAR TOURS: Guided cellar tours are held by arrangement.
WINES:
60/40 ★★★
Rhine Riesling ★★(★)
Sainte Dominique ★★(★)
Sauvignon Blanc ★★(★)
Cabernet Sauvignon (no rating)

FRANSCHHOEK VINEYARDS CO-OPERATIVE

This co-op differs from most in that it does keep certain deliveries of grapes from some of its members separate. These are vinified separately, and the eventual product is then bottled under the label of the vineyards of origin. Most of its crush, however, goes into the co-op's ranges of La Cotte and Franschhoek Vallei Co-op wines. At one time, 10 cents of every case of La Cotte sold went towards the restoration of the historic La Cotte Mill (built in 1779), which was reopened by Dr Anton Rupert in 1989.

The cellar's tasting room cannot be missed as you enter Franschhoek village on the R45 from the lower end of the valley.

ADDRESS: Franschhoek Vineyards Co-op, P. O. Box 52,
Franschhoek 7690
TELEPHONE: (02212) 2086/7

FAX: (02212) 2086/7 and ask for the fax
WINE SALES AND TASTING: Weekdays: 08h30 to 13h00 and 14h00 to 17h30
Saturdays: 09h00 to 13h00
Tasting costs R2-00 for the glass.
CELLAR TOURS: Cellar tours are held by appointment between February and April.
WINES:
La Cotte Rhine Riesling ★★★(★)
Sauvignon Blanc Brut ★★★

La Cotte Chenin Blanc ★★(★)
La Cotte Sauvignon Blanc ★★(★)
La Cotte Sémillon ★★(★)
La Cotte Claret ★★
La Cotte Hárslevelü ★★
La Cotte Red Port ★★
La Cotte Sweet Hanepoot ★★
Premier Grand Rouge ★★
Sparkling Wine ★★
La Cotte Pinotage Blanc de Noir ★(★)
La Cotte Cabernet ★
Light (★)
La Cotte Port (no rating)

HAUTE PROVENCE

This farm is owned by foreign correspondent Peter Younghusband, and the wines are made at the Franschhoek Co-op.

ADDRESS: Haute Provence, P. O. Box 211, Franschhoek 7690
TELEPHONE: (02212) 3195
WINE SALES AND TASTING: Tastings are held from 15 December to 15 April
Weekdays 14h00 to 16h00
Saturdays 10h00 to 12h00
Visitors are welcome at other times by appointment. No wines are sold at Haute Provence, though they

may be bought at the Franschhoek Vineyards Co-op.
CELLAR TOURS: No cellar tours.
WINES:
Blanc Fumé ★★★
Brut ★★(★)
Grand Vin Blanc ★★(★)
Larmes des Anges ★★(★)
Blanc Royale (no rating)
Chardonnay (no rating)

LA BRI

La Bri is owned by Michael and Cheryl Trull, who have played a dynamic role in the Franschhoek renaissance. Michael, as original chairman of the Vignerons de Franschhoek, was the driving force behind the highly successful marketing concept. Now developing

Ornate large barrels help to give the cellar at La Motte an air of history.

vineyards in England, the Trulls spend South African summers in the Cape, and Northern Hemisphere summers in England.

ADDRESS: La Bri, Franschhoek 7690
TELEPHONE: (02212) 2593

WINE SALES AND TASTING: Visits to La Bri are by appointment only.

LA MOTTE

Owned by Paul Neethling (son in law of Anton Rupert) this estate – the first of the Bergkelder estates to bottle on the premises – has proved that Franschhoek can indeed produce excellent red wines. General opinion was that the Franschhoek valley was very much a white wine area only. However, La Motte's rich, deep Shirazes and Cabernet Sauvignons have proved this to be untrue. Existing buildings have been beautifully restored and a modern cellar has been built to blend well with the old.

ADDRESS: La Motte Estate, P. O. Box 45, La Motte 7691
TELEPHONE: (02212) 3119

WINE SALES AND TASTING: Visitors by appointment only.

LA PROVENCE

Owned by international businessman, John Rudd, this farm now has its wines made at the Franschhoek Co-op. Look for the Vignerons de Franschoek sign for La Provence on the R45, and you will come to the cellar about a kilometre off the road.

ADDRESS: La Provence, P. O. Box 188, Franschhoek 7690
TELEPHONE: (02212) 2163
WINE SALES AND TASTING: Weekdays: 09h00 to 12h00
Otherwise by appointment only.

Tastings are free of charge.
CELLAR TOURS: No cellar tours.
WINES:
La Valle Vin Doux ★★★
Blanc Fleuri ★★
Cuvée Blanche ★★

L'ORMARINS

This estate, on the slopes of Groot Drakenstein, is renowned for its full reds and well-flavoured whites. The farm is owned by Antonij Rupert, youngest son of well-known businessman Anton Rupert, and the wine maker is Nico Vermeulen. The historic Cape Dutch homestead and old cellar have been perfectly restored. Behind the old cellar is an ultra-modern cellar where the wine is made with the most advanced technology available .

ADDRESS: L'Ormarins Estate, Private Bag, Suider-Paarl 7624
TELEPHONE: (02211) 4 1024
WINE SALES AND TASTING: The wines are marketed by the

Bergkelder so there are no sales on the estate, however visitors are welcome on weekdays from 09h00 to 17h00 or by appointment.

MOUTON EXCELSIOR

Mouton Excelsior is owned by coal-mining magnate, Ben Mouton. The tasting room is behind the Swiss Farm Excelsior Hotel. In the past, wines were bought and labelled 'Le Moutonné'. Now, grapes from the farm's own vineyards will be made into wine in redeveloped cellars on the premises. Also, the range of wines will be extended.

ADDRESS: Mouton Excelsior, P. O. Box 290, Franschhoek 7690
TELEPHONE: (02212) 3316
WINE SALES AND TASTING:
Weekdays: 09h00 to 17h00
Saturdays: 10h00 to 14h00
A tasting is also held at 12h00 on Sundays. Tastings cost R2-50 a head.
CELLAR TOURS: There are no cellar tours.
RESTAURANT: From December to April, throughout the week, Die

Binnehof serves cheese platters (R12-50) and picnic lunches (R45-00 a two-person basket) which can be eaten in the gardens outside. Booking for the picnic lunches is essential.
WINES:
Cabernet Sauvignon ★★★
Sémillon ★★
Le Moutonné (Chardonnay) (no rating)
Le Moutonné (Merlot) (no rating)

The neo-classical gable of the L'Ormarins homestead is reflected in an ornamental lake.
The farm was originally granted to Huguenot refugee Jean Roi in 1694.

Worcester

The new Huguenot tunnel through the Dutoitskloof mountains makes the Breede River valley just that much more accessible. The Worcester Wineland Association (0231) 2 8710 will help you plan your visit to get the most out of this large, sprawling area. The Worcester Wine Route stretches from Romansrivier in the north down the Breede River to Rondebosch, and from Villiersdorp near Somerset West to De Doorns at the head of the Hex River Valley. This is a large area, with greatest concentration of cellars being in the Slanghoek-Dutoitskloof-Rawsonville-Goudini area.

As you leave Worcester on the road to Robertson, you will see the Kleinplasie complex of agricultural showgrounds, where the Worcester Wineland Association have their offices. The Kleinplasie Restaurant features traditional Cape cooking, while wines from the local cellars can be tasted and purchased at the wine house. Accommodation is also available here.

On the same premises is the Open Air Farm Museum, where visitors can see a number of fascinating traditional farm activities – such as tobacco twisting, bread baking in old-style mud ovens, and the distillation of Witblits – taking place.

There is a range of accommodation available in and around the town of Worcester; contact your local tourist information bureau for further information.

AAN-DE-DOORNS CO-OPERATIVE

This co-op lies eight kilometres outside Worcester, on the R43 – which goes from Worcester to Villiersdorp. It was established in 1954, and today has some 45 members supplying about 14 000 tons of grapes annually.

ADDRESS: Aan-de-Doorns Co-op,
P. O. Box 235, Worcester 6850
TELEPHONE: (0231) 7 2301
WINE SALES AND TASTING:
Weekdays: 08h30 to 12h00 and
13h00 to 17h30
Saturdays: 08h00 to 12h00
Tastings are free of charge.
CELLAR TOURS: Guided cellar tours are held by appointment, are limited to approximately 15 people and take about one hour.
WINES:
Chenin Blanc ★★★

Muscat d'Alexandrie ★★★
Cabernet Sauvignon ★★
Colombar ★★
Dry Red ★★
Laatoes Steen ★★
Pinotage ★★
Premier Grand Crû ★★
Riesling ★★
Spesiale Laatoes Steen ★★
Vin Rouge ★★
Clairette Blanche ★(★)
Port ★(★)
Sauvignon Blanc ★(★)
Vin Rosé ★

AUFWAERTS CO-OPERATIVE

The co-op lies 19 kilometres outside Worcester, near Rawsonville on the N1 to Cape Town.

ADDRESS: Aufwaerts Co-op,
P. O. Box 51, Rawsonville 6845
TELEPHONE: (0231) 9 1750/1513
WINE SALES AND TASTING: Wine sales and tasting are available on request.
CELLAR TOURS: Guided cellar tours are held by appointment.

BADSBERG CO-OPERATIVE

Badsberg Co-op can be found close to the Rondalia Holiday Resort at Goudini. It was established in 1951, beginning wine making the following year, and crushes about 13 000 tons of grapes annually. The co-op produces a very good Hanepoot, and a limited range of natural wines and grape juice.

ADDRESS: Badsberg Co-op,
P. O. Box 72, Rawsonville 6845
TELEPHONE: (0231) 9 1120
WINE SALES AND TASTING:
Weekdays: 09h00 to 12h00 and
13h00 to 17h00

The variety of autumn colours in the vineyards, and the snow-capped mountains, make the Hex River valley an exceptionally beautiful part of the Cape winelands.

Saturdays: 09h00 to 12h00 Tastings are free of charge unless large groups are involved (snacks are provided for such groups).
CELLAR TOURS: Guided cellar tours are held Mondays to Saturdays at 11h00.
WINES:
Hanepoot ★★★★ This cellar produces an excellent, full, sweet and golden Hanepoot: a remarkable wine which has gained numerous awards at regional and national shows. It is also a consistent gold-medal and trophy winner at the South African Championship Wine Show and has carried Superior certification for almost every vintage since 1974.
Badlese ★★
Riesling ★★
Sauvignon Blanc ★★
Servan Blanc ★★
Stein ★(★)
Tafelwyn ★(★)

lots of complexity and is lovely as a young wine, but should also develop well.
Noble Late Harvest ★★★(★)
Bukettraube Special Late Harvest ★★★
Cabernet Sauvignon ★★★
Chenin Blanc Special Late Harvest ★★★
Colombard ★★★
Fernão Pires ★★★
Furmint ★★★
Pinotage ★★★
Riesling ★★★
Sauvignon Blanc ★★★
Sweet Hanepoot ★★★
Weisser Riesling Special Late Harvest ★★★
Bouquet Light ★★(★)
Pinotage Blanc de Noir ★★(★)
Weisser Riesling ★★(★)
Gewürztraminer ★★
Port ★★

BERGSIG

Bergsig, one of the few estates in the area, is owned by former Springbok, 'Prop' Lategan. It lies 29 kilometres outside Worcester, on the R43 to Ceres. The estate is made up of six farms, but less than two per cent of the grapes end up as wine bottled under the Bergsig label.

Over the years Bergsig has made some excellent Special and Noble Late Harvests. The estate produces a wide range of types and styles of wine, from good Cabernet through a range of cultivars which include unusual names like Fernão Pires and Furmint. A Blanc de Noir bubbly has recently been introduced.

ADDRESS: Bergsig Estate, P. O. Box 15, Breede River 6858
TELEPHONE: (02324) 603
WINE SALES AND TASTING:
Weekdays: 08h45 to 16h45
Saturdays: 09h00 to 12h00
Tastings are free of charge.

CELLAR TOURS: No cellar tours.
WINES:
Gewürztraminer Special Late Harvest ★★★★ This is Bergsig's best wine from the 1989 vintage. It is well made with intense flavours of peaches and tropical fruits. It has

BOTHA CO-OPERATIVE

The co-op is situated on the R43, 20 kilometres on the Ceres side of Worcester, close to the Breede River. It was established in 1949, and now has some 45 members. Well known for its value-for-money Cabernet, the co-op produces both cultivar and fortified wines.

ADDRESS: Botha Co-op, P. O. Botha 6857
TELEPHONE: (02324) 740
WINE SALES AND TASTING:
Weekdays: 08h30 to 12h30 and 13h30 to 17h30
Saturdays: 10h00 to 12h00
Tastings are free of charge.
CELLAR TOURS: No cellar tours.
WINES:
Cabernet Sauvignon ★★★
Colombard ★★★
Pinotage ★★★
Soet Hanepoot ★★★
Blanc de Noir ★★
Chenin Blanc ★★
Chenin Blanc Late Harvest ★★
Droë Rooiwyn ★★
Portwyn ★★
Riesling ★★
Weisser Riesling ★★

BRANDVLEI CO-OPERATIVE

Established in 1954, this 40-member co-op crushes some 14 000 tons of grapes annually. It is situated 23 kilometres from Worcester off the R43, en route to Villiersdorp. The original site was flooded by the extensions to the Brandvlei dam, and the co-op was rebuilt on its present site in 1974. Like most co-ops, Brandvlei sends the bulk of its production to merchants, but a small quantity is bottled for sale at the winery.

ADDRESS: Brandvlei Co-op,
P. O. Box 595, Worcester 6850
TELEPHONE: (0231) 9 4215
WINE SALES AND TASTING: Sales
Weekdays: 08h30 to 12h30 and
13h30 to 17h00
Tastings are available for groups by appointment.
CELLAR TOURS: Guided cellar tours are held by appointment.

WINES:
Chenel ★★
Colombar ★★
Grand Crû ★★
Laat Oes ★★
Port ★★
Soet Hanepoot ★★
Stein ★★
Dry Red (no rating)

DE DOORNS CO-OPERATIVE

The De Doorns Co-operative wine cellar is situated outside the village of De Doorns in the Hex River valley. Just off the N1 (30 kilometres from Worcester), this is the first cellar in the western Cape that travellers arriving at the Cape from the north encounter. The co-op was established in 1968, and today has a huge membership of over 200 farms.

The co-operative crushes both wine grapes and table grapes which are not suitable for the market, and are consequently used for distilling: tonnage can vary from 25 000 to nearly 32 000. It also packs large quantitites of table grapes for export for its members.

The first wines bottled under the co-op's label were released in 1977, and today wine maker Pieter Hamman is responsible for a full range of about a dozen wines including Perlés and Sparklings – prices are deliberately kept low.

ADDRESS: De Doorns Co-op,
P. O. Box 129, De Doorns 6875
TELEPHONE: (02322) 2100 •
WINE SALES AND TASTING:
Weekdays: 08h00 to 12h30 and
13h30 to 17h00
Saturdays: 08h00 to 12h00
Tastings are available for those who wish to buy. They are free of charge.
CELLAR TOURS: Guided cellar tours are held by appointment.
WINES:
Grand Crû ★★
Grand Rouge ★★
Pinotage ★★
Port ★★
Roodehof ★★
Stein ★★
Colombar ★
Laatoes ★
Sauvignon Blanc ★
Sparkling Wine ★
Hanepoot (no rating)
Perlé Blanc (no rating)
Perlé Rosé (no rating)

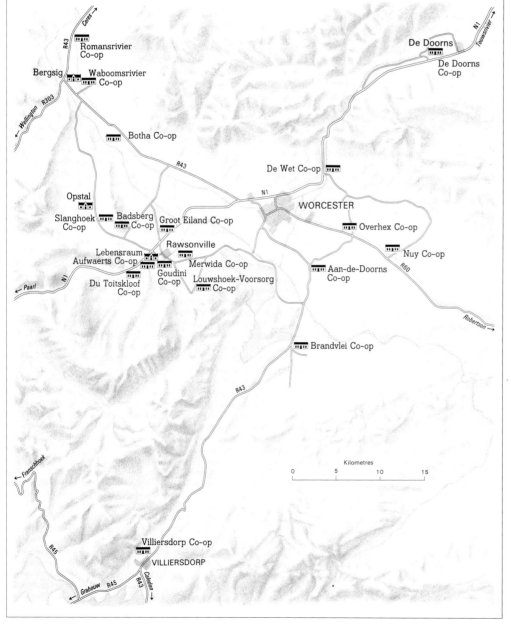

Vineyards run right next to the railway line at De Wet.

DE WET CO-OPERATIVE

De Wet Co-op was established in 1946, and its 50 members deliver about 15 000 tons of grapes annually. It is situated at the lower end of the Hex River Valley, eight kilometres from Worcester, on the N1.

ADDRESS: De Wet Co-op,
P. O. Box 16, De Wet 6853
TELEPHONE: (0231) 9 2710
WINE SALES AND TASTING:
Weekdays: 08h00 to 17h00
Saturdays: 09h00 to 12h00
Tastings are free of charge.
CELLAR TOURS: Guided tours of the co-operative's cellars are held by appointment.

WINES:
Muscats ★★(★)
Riesling ★★(★)
Blanc de Noir ★★
Clairette Blanche ★★
Grand Crû ★★
Kerner ★★
Huiswyn Stein ★
Sauvignon Blanc ★
Sweet Hanepoot (no rating)

DU TOITSKLOOF CO-OPERATIVE

Lying on the Worcester side of the Huguenot Tunnel, 20 kilometres from Worcester on the N1, this co-op presses between 10 000 and 12 000 tons from only 10 members.

The quality of Du Toitskloof's wines has improved in recent years, as has their presentation. The co-op now produces a large range of award-winning wines, some of which are very good value for money. The Special Late Harvests and Hanepoots are consistently good.

ADDRESS: Du Toitskloof Co-op,
P. O. Box 55, Rawsonville 6845
TELEPHONE: (0231) 9 1601
WINE SALES AND TASTING:
Weekdays: 08h30 to 12h30 and 13h30 to 17h30
Saturdays: 08h30 to 12h00
Tastings are free of charge.
CELLAR TOURS: Guided cellar tours are held by appointment.
WINES:
Bukettraube ★★★(★)
Chenin Blanc ★★★(★)
Red Jerepigo ★★★(★)
Blanc de Blanc ★★★

Blanc de Noir ★★★
Cinsaut ★★★
Colombard ★★★
Hanepoot Jerepigo ★★★
Late Vintage ★★★
Muscat d'Alexandrie ★★★
Noble Late Harvest ★★★
Port ★★★
Riesling ★★★
Soet Hanepoot ★★★
Sparkling Wine ★★★
Special Late Harvest ★★★
Sauvignon Blanc ★★(★)
Weisser Riesling ★★(★)
Cinet (★)

GOUDINI CO-OPERATIVE

Ten kilometres from Worcester, just past Rawsonville on the road to the Brandvlei dam, lies the Goudini Co-op. Established in 1948, it usually crushes about 16 000 tons of grapes annually. The co-op produces a consistently outstanding, award-winning fortified Hanepoot.

ADDRESS: Goudini Co-op,
P. O. Box 132, Rawsonville 6845
TELEPHONE: (0231) 9 1090
WINE SALES AND TASTING:
Weekdays: 08h00 to 12h00 and 13h00 to 17h00
Tastings are held on request.
CELLAR TOURS: Guided cellar tours are held by appointment.
WINES:
Soet Hanepoot ★★★★ Previously called Muscat d'Alexandrie. A regular medal and trophy winner at local and national shows, it is
always full and sweet, with plenty of fruit flavour. Wines such as this one deserve to be better known. The 1988 is really super.
Steen Noble Late Harvest ★★★(★)
Steen Late Harvest ★★(★)
Chenin Blanc ★★
Clairette Blanche ★★
Pinotage ★★
Premier Grand Crû ★★
Riesling ★★
Sauvignon Blanc ★★
Red Dessert ★(★)

The Breede River meanders slowly past the town of Worcester, on its way from the Elandskloofberge to the Indian Ocean.

GROOT EILAND CO-OPERATIVE

Established in 1961, this co-op has only 14 members. It is situated 16 kilometres from Worcester, just off the road that links Rawsonville with the Worcester/Ceres road, and close to the Breede River.

ADDRESS: Groot Eiland Co-op,
P. O. Box 93, Rawsonville 6845
TELEPHONE: (0231) 9 1140
WINE SALES AND TASTING:
Weekdays: 08h30 to 12h30 and 14h00 to 17h00
Tastings are free of charge.
CELLAR TOURS: Guided cellar tours are held Mondays to Fridays by appointment. They are limited to 20 people and last approximately
30 minutes.
WINES:
Hanepoot Soetwyn ★★(★)
Bukettraube ★★
Chenin Blanc ★★
Laatoes Steen ★★
Port ★★
Riesling ★★
Cinsaut ★(★)
Wit Tafelwyn ★

LEBENSRAUM

Lebensraum Estate lies 16 kilometres from Worcester, just off the N1 near Rawsonville, and has been owned by the Deetleefs since 1822.

ADDRESS: Lebensraum Estate,
P. O. Box 36, Rawsonville 6845
TELEPHONE: (0231) 9 1137/1260
WINE SALES AND TASTING:
Weekdays: 14h00 to 18h00
Tastings are held on request.
Cellar tours: Guided cellar tours are
held by appointment and limited to 15 people. They last one hour.
WINES:
Soet Hanepoot ★★★(★)
Weisser Riesling ★★(★)
Cape Riesling (no rating)

LOUWSHOEK-VOORSORG CO-OPERATIVE

This co-op was established in 1956, and crushes 13 000 tons of grapes a year, received from its 30 members. It lies 17 kilometres from Worcester, on the road from Rawsonville to Brandvlei dam.

The co-op produces an aperitif called Nectar de Privision, which is similar to the Pineau des Charentes, and made from Colombar fortified with brandy and aged for two years. Drink chilled.

ADDRESS: Louwshoek-Voorsorg
Co-op, P. O. Box 174,
Rawsonville 6845
TELEPHONE: (0231) 9 1110
WINE SALES AND TASTING:
Weekdays: 08h30 to 12h30
Saturdays: 09h00 to 12h00
There are no tastings.
CELLAR TOURS: Guided cellar tours are held by appointment, and they last one hour.

WINES:
Muscat d'Alexandrie ★★★
Nectar de Provision ★★★
Colombar ★★
Noble Late Harvest ★★
Dry Red ★
Riesling ★
Chenin Blanc (no rating)
Laatoes (no rating)
Premier Grand Crû (no rating)

MERWIDA CO-OPERATIVE

Merwida is situated 10 kilometres from Worcester, near Louwshoek. It is a family concern of the Van der Merwes, with only two members – although they comprise seven farms totalling 700 hectares. It presses over 5 000 tons of grapes annually.

ADDRESS: Merwida Co-op,
P. O. Box 4, Rawsonville 6845
TELEPHONE: (0231) 9 1301
WINES SALES AND TASTING:
Weekdays: 08h30 to 12h00 and
13h30 to 17h30
Tastings are free of charge.
CELLAR TOURS: Guided tours of the co-operative's cellars are held by appointment.

WINES:
Colombar ★★★
Riesling ★★(★)
Chenin Blanc ★★
Fernão Pires ★★
Pinotage ★★
Tafelwyn ★★
Hanepoot ★
Port ★
Sauvignon Blanc ★

NUY CO-OPERATIVE

This is one of the more curious names in the wine world – it is pronounced 'Nay'. The cellar is situated in the foothills of the Kwadousberg, and the turn off for it is on the left of the R60, 22 kilometres from Worcester as you head towards Robertson.

Established in 1963, and crushing about 8 000 tons annually from 21 members, this co-op has a remarkable record of quality success, especially with its tremendous fortified Muscadels. It also produces excellent Colombars and a most unusual wine called Chant de Nuy.

ADDRESS: Nuy Wine Cellar,
P. O. Box 5225, Worcester 6850
TELEPHONE: (0231) 7 0272
WINE SALES AND TASTING:
Weekdays: 08h30 to 16h30
Saturdays: 08h30 to 12h30
Tastings are free of charge.
CELLAR TOURS: Guided cellar tours are held by appointment during harvest time (February to March).
WINES:
Red Muscadel ★★★★★ One of the best sweet Red Muscadels made in

South Africa: light, not full-sweet, and showing the Hanepoot character at its best. A consistent award-winner at regional and national shows, it has twice been judged champion Muscat at the South African Championship Wine Show, and every vintage carries Superior certification.
Chant de Nuy ★★★★ This is a very good blend of Colombar and Steen, with a touch of something that produces a finely flavoured, bone

dry, white wine with a most appealing pineapple nose coming from a grape called Ferdinand de Lesseps. Despite its dryness, it is soft across the palate, with a good clean finish.
Colombard ★★★★ This wine is fairly tart, with a full cultivar nose and good full flavour.
Colombard Effesoet ★★★★ This is fuller in the mouth than Nuy's other Colombard, and usually the finer wine: it develops well in the bottle and is consistently one of the better

Colombars. The 1989 is a little below the usual standard.
White Muscadel ★★★★ This has the same high quality as the Nuy Red, but it does not achieve the other's peaks. Nevertheless, it is a regular medal and class winner at regional and national shows.
Bukettraube ★★★
Effesoet Steen ★★★
Fernão Pires ★★★
Pinotage ★★★
Riesling ★★★
Steen Laat Oes ★★★

OPSTAL

Opstal Estate in the Slanghoek Valley is 30 kilometres from Worcester, and is owned by the Louw family. It first began bottling in 1978. Each year, on the last Saturday in February, a Harvest Day is held, at which the public can harvest baskets of grapes themselves. The grapes are then loaded onto tractors and taken to the cellar, where the crushing and sorting processes can be seen. This is followed by a braai lunch. Booking is essential.

ADDRESS: Opstal Estate,
P. O. Box 27, Rawsonville 6845
TELEPHONE: (0231) 9 1066
WINE SALES AND TASTING:
Weekdays: 09h00 to 11h00 and
14h00 to 17h00
Tastings are free of charge.
CELLAR TOURS: Guided cellar and farm tours are held on Mondays, Wednesdays and Fridays by appointment.

RESTAURANT: Light lunches can be arranged by appointment for 10 to 20 people.
WINES:
Blanc de Noir ★★★
Colombar ★★★
Weisser Riesling ★★★
Steen ★★(★)
Volsoet Hanepoot ★★(★)
Chenin Blanc ★

OVERHEX CO-OPERATIVE

On the R60, seven kilometres from Worcester on the way to Robertson, lies the Overhex Co-op, which was established in 1964. Sixteen members deliver over 8 000 tons of grapes annually. A small range of wines is on sale at the cellar.

ADDRESS: Overhex Co-op,
P. O. Box 139, Worcester 6850
TELEPHONE: (0231) 7 1057
WINE SALES AND TASTING:
Weekdays: 09h00 to 13h00 and
14h00 to 17h00
No tasting (though there are plans to introduce this from July 1991).

CELLAR TOURS: No cellar tours (though there are plans to introduce this from July 1991).
WINES:
Effesoet Colombard ★★(★)
Droë Wit Tafelwyn ★★
Riesling ★★

ROMANSRIVIER CO-OPERATIVE

Romansrivier Co-op lies at the lower end of the Tulbagh Valley, 40 kilometres from Worcester. Established in 1949 – through the efforts of two local farmers, H. F. Conradie and D. J. Viljoen – it crushes between 10 000 and 12 000 tons of grapes annually, which it receives from its 65 members. The co-op consistently produces good value-for-money wines, including some very good Noble Late Harvests.

Romansrivier also has a depot at Ceres, on the Eselfontein Road. The depot is open on Tuesdays and Fridays (08h30 to 12h00 and 13h30 to 17h00) for sales only.

Summer turns the vineyards of the Hex River valley a lush green. the Worcester wine region is considered a hot area, but snow often tops the mountains in winter.

ADDRESS: Romansrivier Co-op,
P. O. Box 108, Wolseley 6830
TELEPHONE: (0236) 31 1070
WINE SALES AND TASTING:
 Weekdays: 08h30 to 12h00 and
13h30 to 17h00
Saturdays: 08h30 to 10h30
CELLAR TOURS: Guided cellar tours
are held by appointment. They are
limited to 20 people and last
between 30 minutes and an hour.
WINES:
Edel Laatoes ★★★(★)
Cabernet Sauvignon ★★★
Colombard ★★★
Special Late Harvest ★★★
Stein ★★★

Vin Blanc Special Reserve ★★★
Vino Rood ★★★
Chenel ★★(★)
Pinotage ★★(★)
Port ★★(★)
Riesling ★★(★)
Blanc de Blanc ★★
Blanc de Noir ★★
Grand Crû ★★
Sauvignon Blanc ★★
Vin Doux ★★
Chenin Blanc (no rating)
Hanepoot (no rating)
Late Harvest (no rating)
Nouveau (no rating)
Rosé (no rating)

SLANGHOEK CO-OPERATIVE

In the Slanghoek Valley, 30 kilometres from Worcester, lies the Slanghoek Co-op. It was established in 1951, and has 33 members that deliver 18 000 to 20 000 tons of grapes annually.

The co-op makes a full range of wines, of which the Soet Hanepoot is a consistent award winner.

ADDRESS: Slanghoek Co-op,
P. O. Box 75, Rawsonville 6845
TELEPHONE: (0231) 9 1130
WINE SALES AND TASTING:
Mondays to Thursdays: 09h00 to
12h30 and 13h30 to 17h30
Fridays: 09h00 to 12h30 and 13h30
to 16h30
Saturdays: 10h00 to 12h00
Tastings are free of charge.
CELLAR TOURS: Guided cellar tours

are held by appointment for
groups of not less than 25 people.
WINES:
Soet Hanepoot ★★★(★)
Chenin Blanc ★★★
Colombard ★★★
Pinotage ★★★
Late Harvest ★★
Premier grand Crû ★★
Sauvignon Blanc ★★
Riesling ★★

VILLIERSDORP CO-OPERATIVE

This co-op began in 1922 and the original intention was to concentrate on the production of *moskonfyt* and processed fruits. Villiersdorp was expanded to include wine production in 1976, and the first bottling took place in 1978. Today, it has over 100 members and crushes 10 000 tons of grapes annually. It is situated 50 kilometres from Worcester, on the R43, right in the town of Villiersdorp.

ADDRESS: Villiersdorp Co-op,
P. O. Box 14, Villiersdorp 7170
TELEPHONE: (0225) 3 1120
WINE SALES AND TASTING:
Weekdays: 08h00 to 17h00
Saturdays: 08h30 to 11h00
Wine may be tasted: tastings are
free of charge.
CELLAR TOURS: Guided tours of the
co-operative's cellars are held by
appointment.

WINES:
Blanc de Blanc ★★
Chenin Blanc ★★
Colombar ★★
Grand Crû ★★
Hanepoot Jerepigo ★★
Pinotage ★★
Sauvignon Blanc ★
Special Late Harvest ★
Blanc de Noir (no rating)
Late Vintage (no rating)

WABOOMSRIVIER CO-OPERATIVE

Established in 1949, this co-op has 45 members delivering 10 000 to 11 000 tons of grapes to it annually. It produces consistently good value-for-money wines, including an unusual Ruby Cabernet. It is situated 25 kilometres from Worcester on the R43 to Ceres.

ADDRESS: Waboomsrivier Co-op,
P. O. Box 24, Breede River 6858
TELEPHONE: (02324) 730/1
WINE SALES AND TASTING:
Weekdays: 08h30 to 12h30 and
13h30 to 17h00
Saturdays: 08h30 to 10h00

Tastings are free of charge.
CELLAR TOURS: Guided cellar tours
are held by appointment.
WINES:
Wagenboom Cabernet Sauvignon
★★★
Port ★★(★)

Robertson

Less than two hours drive from Cape Town lies the scenic Robertson wine region. The area includes the districts of Ashton, Bonnievale, McGregor and Robertson, and is renowned for its wine, brandy, champion horses, cheese and beautiful roses. The lovely Breede River flows through the area, and is the venue for one of the country's major annual double canoe marathons.

The Robertson Wine Trust (tel. (02351) 3167) was established in 1983, and represents 25 cellars. The information centre for the trust is housed at Branewynsdraai in the town of Robertson. Branewynsdraai is also the home of a restaurant (Tel. (02351) 3202) that caters for breakfast, lunch, teas, and dinner, and sells wines and souvenirs.

On the main road through the town of Robertson are two wine co-ops and one of the world's largest wine and brandy distilleries. There is a range of accommodation in and around Robertson, and some very pleasant places in McGregor. Contact your local tourist information bureau for further information.

AGTERKLIPHOOGTE CO-OPERATIVE

Some 28 kilometres from Robertson, in a valley to the north of the Riviersonderend Mountains, lies the Agterkliphoogte Co-op. It was established in 1966, and now has 24 members. The co-op employs night harvesting for its Colombar, and also makes an Emerald Riesling.

ADDRESS: Agterkliphoogte Wine Cellar, P. O. Box 267, Robertson 6705
TELEPHONE: (02351) 6 1103
WINE SALES AND TASTING:
 Weekdays: 08h30 to 12h30 and 13h30 to 17h00
CELLAR TOURS: Guided cellar tours are held by appointment.
WINES:
Colombar ★★
Muscadel ★★
Chenin Blanc ★
Emerald Riesling (no rating)
Soet Hanepoot (no rating)

ASHTON CO-OPERATIVE

Established in 1962, this co-op has a large membership of about 90 who deliver over 20 000 tons of grapes each harvest.

Situated just outside Ashton on the road to Robertson, it has a modern grape-concentrating operation, and, in some vintages, almost half the crop is concentrated. The cellar makes a full range of wines, including some good cultivar wines.

ADDRESS: Ashton Co-op,
P. O. Box 40, Ashton 6715
TELEPHONE: (0234) 5 1135
WINE SALES AND TASTING:
Weekdays: 08h00 to 12h30 and 13h30 to 17h30

Goedemoed, the elegant and historic homestead at Bon Courage, was built in 1818.

The neatly regimented rows of vines create interesting patterns for the motorist passing this farm near the small town of Bonnievale in the Breede River valley.

Tastings are free of charge.
CELLAR TOURS: Guided cellar tours are held by appointment.
WINES:
Rooi Muskadel ★★★(★)
Bukettraube ★★★
Cabernet Sauvignon ★★★
Dry Red ★★★
Petillant Blanc ★★★
Wit Muskadel ★★★
Blanc Fumé ★★
Colombar ★★
Gewürztraminer ★★
Hanepoot ★★
Laat Oes ★★
Spesiale Laatoes ★★

BON COURAGE

Situated nine kilometres from Robertson, on the road to Bonnievale, this estate lies on the northern bank of the Breede River, at its confluence with the Klaasvoogds River. It was once part of the larger property of Goedemoed (Bon Courage is in fact a French translation of Goedemoed), which has been in the Bruwer family since the 1920s. Registered as an estate in 1980, Bon Courage has a long list of show successes culminating in 1990 with the Diners Club Award for Winemaker of the Year with a 1989 Gewürztraminer Special Late Harvest.

The estate makes a full range of wines, including a consistently good Special Late Harvest and Red Muscadel Jerepigo.

ADDRESS: Bon Courage Estate, P. O. Box 589, Robertson 6705
TELEPHONE: (02351) 4557 (if no reply 4170/8)
WINE SALES AND TASTING:
Weekdays: 08h00 to 12h00 and
14h00 to 17h00
Saturdays: 09h00 to 12h00
Tastings are free of charge.
CELLAR TOURS: Guided tours of the estate's wine cellars are held by appointment.

WINES:
Bouquet Blanc ★★★(★)
Kerner Special Late Harvest
★★★(★)
Noble Late Harvest ★★★(★)
Red Muscadel Jerepigo ★★★(★)
Blanc de Noir ★★★
Chardonnay ★★★
White Muscadel Jerepigo ★★★
Blanc Fumé ★★(★)
Gewürztraminer ★★(★)
Riesling ★★(★)
Weisser Riesling ★★(★)
Kerner Late Harvest ★★
Sauvignon Blanc ★★
Gewürztraminer Special Late Harvest (no rating)

BONNIEVALE CO-OPERATIVE

Two kilometres outside Bonnievale, on the road to Stormsvlei, is this 50-member co-op that crushes some 13 000 tons annually. Most of the production goes in bulk to the merchants, but each year six or so wines are bottled for sale to the public. Their natural Colombar and fortified Hanepoot are consistently good.

ADDRESS: Bonnievale Co-op, P. O. Box 206, Bonnievale 6730
TELEPHONE: (02346) 2795
WINE SALES AND TASTING:
Weekdays: 08h30 to 12h30 and 13h30 to 17h00
CELLAR TOURS: Guided cellar tours are held by appointment.

WINES:
Late Vintage ★★(★)
Colombard ★★
Pinotage ★★
Chenin Blanc (no rating)
Colombard Effesoet (no rating)
Hanepoot Jerepigo (no rating)

CLAIRVAUX CO-OPERATIVE

Clairvaux is situated on the outskirts of Robertson, on the main road to Worcester. This is a 16 member co-op, established in 1963, which crushes a little over 2 500 tons of grapes annually. The original cellar dates back to 1910, but it has been consistently modernized in recent times. The cellar sports an external mural showing the journey of wine from grapes to bottle to glass.

The co-op produces a full range of wine.

ADDRESS: Clairvaux Co-op,
P. O. Box 179, Robertson 6705
TELEPHONE: (02351) 3842
WINE SALES AND TASTING:
Weekdays: 08h30 to 12h30 and
13h30 to 17h30
Saturdays: 08h30 to 12h30
Tastings are free of charge.
CELLAR TOURS: There are no
cellar tours.

WINES:
Special Late Harvest ★★(★)
Cabernet Sauvignon ★★
Goue Jerepigo ★★
Pinotage ★★
Port ★★
Red Muskadel Jerepigo ★★
Rhine Riesling ★★
White Muskadel ★★
Blanc de Noir ★

DE WETSHOF

Seventeen kilometres east of Robertson, on the R317, lying at the confluence of the Breede and Cogmanskloof rivers is the pioneering estate of De Wetshof. Owned by the De Wets since 1952, the estate has an enviable record of innovation, firsts and prestigious awards. It was the first registered estate in the Robertson area, and produced the country's first certified Chardonnay, Sauvignon Blanc and Rhine Riesling. It also achieved the first Superior certifications for Sauvignon Blanc and Chardonnay. To add to all this, De Wetshof has produced the first Noble Late Harvest (Edeloes) in the area.

Although the wines under the De Wetshof label are marketed by the Bergkelder, another range of wines is now available under the Danie de Wet label. A unique third label is being developed for wines that are to be made from vines grown in the stone-wall-enclosed 'Le Clos' vinyard, and will be dedicated to the late Hungarian viticulturist, Desidirius Pongracz.

ADDRESS: De Wetshof Wine Estate,
P. O. Box 31, Robertson 6705
TELEPHONE: (0234) 5 1857/3
WINE SALES AND TASTING:
Weekdays: 09h00 to 12h30 and
14h00 to 17h00
Saturdays: 09h00 to 12h30
Tastings are free of charge.

CELLAR TOURS: Guided cellar tours
are held on request.
WINES:
Chardonnay ★★★(★)
Edeloes ★★★(★)
Rhine Riesling ★★★(★)
Sauvignon Blanc ★★★(★)

LANGVERWACHT CO-OPERATIVE

Langverwacht lies 10 kilometres from Bonnievale, on the road between Robertson and Stormsvlei. Established in 1954, it has over 30 members who deliver nearly 10 000 tons of grapes annually.

The six or so wines that are bottled by the co-operative are all good value-for-money products.

ADDRESS: Langverwacht Co-op,
P. O. Box 87, Bonnievale 6730
TELEPHONE: (02346) 2815
WINE SALES AND TASTING:
Weekdays: 08h00 to 12h30 and
13h30 to 17h00
Tastings are free of charge.
CELLAR TOURS: Guided cellar tours

are held by appointment.
WINES:
Late Harvest ★★
Colombard ★
Colombard Off-dry (no rating)
Hanepoot Jerepigo (no rating)
White Muskadel (no rating)

MCGREGOR CO-OPERATIVE

McGregor Co-operative is situated two kilometres from the picturesque 19th Century village of McGregor in the foothills of the Riviersonderend Mountains, and 17 kilometres from Robertson. It was established in 1948 – producing its first wine in 1950 – and its 46 members usually deliver some 7 500 tons of grapes for pressing annually. However, in 1990 they delivered a record of almost a 1 000 tons more.

The Co-operative makes mainly white wines, though an unusual Blanc de Noir and eventually a Chardonnay and a Cabernet Sauvignon will be available.

ADDRESS: McGregor Co-op, Private
Bag X619, Robertson 6705
TELEPHONE: (02353) 741
WINE SALES AND TASTING:
Weekdays: 08h30 to 12h00 and
13h00 to 17h00
Saturdays by appointment.
Wine may be tasted: tastings free
of charge.
CELLAR TOURS: There are no
cellar tours.

WINES:
Cabernet Sauvignon ★★★
Demi Sec ★★★
Edel Laatoes Steen ★★★)
Red Muscadel ★★★
Blanc de Blanc ★★(★)
Blanc de Noir ★★
Colombar ★★
Laatoes Steen ★★
Rhine Riesling ★★

MERWESPONT CO-OPERATIVE

Seven kilometres down the R317 from Bonnievale, on the northern banks of the Breede River is the Robertson area's most easterly cellar. The original cellar was built here in 1918, but Merwespont co-operative was only established in 1955 – and the building being completed in 1957. The co-op's fifty members deliver some 9 000 tons of grapes each year.

Merwespont bottles a small range of pleasant wines including a Muscat Perlé called Morlé.

ADDRESS: Merwespont Co-op,
P. O. Box 68, Bonnievale 6730
TELEPHONE: (02346) 2800/2734
WINE SALES AND TASTING:
Weekdays: 07h30 to 12h30 and
13h30 to 17h00
Tastings are free of charge.
CELLAR TOURS: Guided tours of the
co-operative's cellars are held

by appointment.
WINES:
Late Vintage ★★
Sauvignon Blanc ★★
Riesling ★
Hanepoot (no rating)
Stein (no rating)
Morlé (no rating)

MON DON

Mon Don is situated 10 kilometres from Robertson, on the road to Bonnievale (R317). The farm has been in the Marais family since the early part of this century. It was purchased by the current owner in 1962, and the name was changed from Goedmoed to Mon Don which means 'my present'. The reason for this was that Hannetjie Marais sold the portion of the farm that she inherited to her son, Pierre, for such a small sum, that it was agreed to give the property a name that described it as a gift.

Since 1983, some of the estate's wine has been bottled for sale to the public. Six or so wines are bottled, with the wine Mystère varying with different vintages. (As the name suggests, the contents are always kept a mystery).

ADDRESS: Mon Don Wine Estate,
P. O. Box 360, Robertson 6705
TELEPHONE: (02351) 4183

WINE SALES AND TASTING:
Visitors by appointment only.

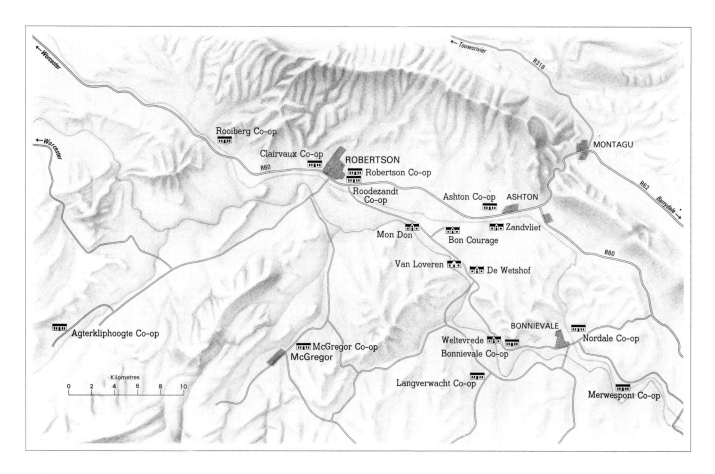

NORDALE CO-OPERATIVE

Just outside Bonnievale, off the road that links Bonnievale to the R60, is the Nordale Co-op. It was established in 1950, and its 40 or so members deliver close to 12 000 tons of grapes annually.

The oldest co-op in the vicinity, it only bottles a fraction of its production, and limits this to between four and six wines each year. Nordale usually produces very good Red Muscadel Jerepigo.

ADDRESS: Nordale Co-op,
P. O. Box 105, Bonnievale 6730
TELEPHONE: (02346) 2050
WINE SALES AND TASTING:
Weekdays: 08h30 to 12h30 and
13h30 to 17h00
Tastings are free of charge.
CELLAR TOURS: Guided cellar tours
are held by appointment.

WINES:
Red Muscadel Jerepigo ★★★★ A
beautiful, rich wine, full of raisins
on the nose.
Nuit St Pierre Blanc de Noir ★★★
Colombard ★★
Late Harvest ★★
Steen ★★

ROBERTSON CO-OPERATIVE

Founded in 1941, this 36-member co-op, which crushes in excess of 20 000 tons of grapes annually, was responsible through the late Pon van Zyl, for making Colombar the 'grape' of the area. The co-op is situated in Constitution Street in Robertson itself.

Special bottlings in memory of Pon van Zyl are done under the label 'Baron du Pon'. To date these have been a Colombar and an outstanding Red Muscadel.

ADDRESS: Robertson Co-op,
P. O. Box 37, Robertson 6705
TELEPHONE: (02351) 3059
WINE SALES AND TASTING:
Mondays to Thursdays: 08h00 to

12h30 and 13h30 to 17h00
Fridays: 08h00 to 12h30 and 13h30
to 16h30
Saturdays: 08h30 to 12h30
Tastings are free of charge.

CELLAR TOURS: Guided cellar tours
are held by appointment.
WINES:
Baron du Pon Red Muscadel ★★★★
The 1986 Red Muscadel is bottled in
magnums and carries a Superior
certification. Only when this cellar
produces an exceptional wine will
it carry the Baron du Pon label.
Bukettraube ★★★(★)

Special Late Harvest ★★★(★)
Baron du Pon ★★★
Blanc de Noir ★★★
Cabernet Sauvignon ★★★
Colombard ★★★
Pinotage ★★★
Robroi ★★★
Sauvignon Blanc ★★★
Soet Muskadel ★★★
Steen Late Vintage ★★

ROODEZANDT CO-OPERATIVE

This co-op is right on the main road through Robertson. It has over 50 members, crushes about 20 000 tons of grapes annually and was founded in 1953.

It produces a large range of natural and fortified wines (25), with outstanding Muscats and some good value-for-money wines, including one of the area's best Cabernet Sauvignons and an unusual Emerald Riesling.

ADDRESS: Roodezandt Co-op,
P. O. Box 164, Robertson 6705
TELEPHONE: (02351) 2912/3020
FAX: (02351) 5074
WINE SALES AND TASTING:
Weekdays: 08h30 to 13h00 and
14h00 to 17h30
Saturdays: 08h30 to 12h30
Tastings are free of charge.
CELLAR TOURS: Guided cellar tours
are held during the harvest time
(February to early April) by
appointment.

WINES:
Hanepoot Jerepigo ★★★★ This
wine is very similar to the Muscat
d'Alexandrie, being light in
character and sweet in flavour.
Muscat d'Alexandrie ★★★★ This
has super Muscat character. It is
quite light, and has a super nose
and lovely sweet flavour.
White Muscadel ★★★★ This is a
traditional full-sweet Muscat, with a
delicious flavour.
Blanc de Blanc ★★★

The elegant buildings of the Roodezandt Co-operative on Voortrekker Street in Robertson are the home of some outstanding fortified sweet wines.

Cabernet Sauvignon ★★★
Chenin Blanc ★★★
Emerald Riesling ★★★
Hoopsrivier Red Muscadelle ★★★
Le Grand Deluge Noble Late
Harvest ★★★
Premier Grand Crû ★★★
Special Late Harvest ★★★
Late Harvest ★★(★)
Pinot Gris ★★(★)
Roode Huiswyn ★★(★)
Sparkling Wine Demi Sec ★★(★)

Blanc de Noir Muscat de
Frontignan ★★
Cape Riesling ★★
Cinsaut ★★
Colombar ★★
Hárslevelü ★★
Port ★★
Sauvignon Blanc ★★
Sparkling Wine Brut ★★
Tinta Barocca ★★
Selected Dry White ★★

ROOIBERG CO-OPERATIVE

Situated 12 kilometres from Robertson on the R60 to Worcester, this is the first Robertson cellar you come to when driving from Worcester. Established in 1964, it has nearly 40 members and crushes between 14 000 and 15 000 tons of grapes annually. The co-op has a remarkable record of achievements, and has been South Africa's champion co-op no fewer than five times.

Rooiberg offers an impressive list of wines, and has a remarkable range of different types and styles, including consistently magnificent fortified Muscats and Late Harvests.

ADDRESS: Rooiberg Co-op, P. O. Box 358, Robertson, 6705
TELEPHONE: (02351) 2312/2322/3146/3147/3148
FAX: (02351) 3295
WINE SALES AND TASTING:
Weekdays: 08h00 to 17h30
Saturdays: 08h00 to 13h00
Tastings are free of charge.
CELLAR TOURS: Guided cellar tours are held on request.
WINES:
Edel Laatoes ★★★★ My first introduction to this wine was from an amazing magnum – this kind of wine is usually bottled in 375-millilitre units. It was from the 1986 vintage and made from Muscat de Frontignan, which shows well, with complexity coming from some botrytis. It is not all that rich and has good acid balance. The 1988 and 1989 are lovely wines, the latter being a blend of 60 per cent Steen and 40 per cent Rhine Riesling.

Red Muscadel ★★★★ A very good, deep-red Muscadel which is always reliable. It is a regular gold-medal winner at local and national shows.
Blanc Fumé Sur Lie ★★★(★)
Colombard ★★★(★)
Port ★★★(★)
Riverside Oak Matured Sauvignon Blanc ★★★(★)
Vinkrivier Chenin Blanc ★★★(★)
Vinkrivier Riesling ★★★(★)
White Muscadel ★★★(★)
Blanc de Noir ★★★
Brut ★★★
Cabernet Sauvignon ★★★
Late Vintage ★★★
Oak Matured Riesling ★★★
Pinotage ★★★
Premier Grand Crû ★★★
Selected Dry White ★★★
Shiraz ★★★
Special Late Harvest ★★★
Vinkrivier Oak Matured Sauvignon Blanc ★★★
White Hanepoot ★★★
Chenin Blanc ★★(★)

Cinsaut ★★(★)
Demi Sec ★★(★)
Pinot Noir ★★(★)
Rosé ★★(★)
Selected Red ★★(★)
Goreë Riesling ★★
Rhine Riesling ★★

Roodewyn ★★
Sauvignon Blanc ★★
Stein ★★
Vinkrivier Bukettraube ★★
Robertson Vintage Reserve (no rating)

VAN LOVEREN

Van Loveren is situated 15 kilometres from Robertson on the road to Bonnievale. It is almost opposite De Wetshof, also at the confluence of the Cogmanskloof and Breede rivers. Van Loveren was originally named Goudmyn F – a section of the larger farm, Goudmyn, bought for Hennie Retief in 1937. The farm remains in the family to this day, and was given its new name by Hennie's wife Jean – her ancestor, Guillaume van Zyl arrived at the Cape in 1692 with his wife, Christina van Loveren.

This innovative cellar, set in attractive gardens, has a delightful rondawel as a tasting room in the middle of the garden. They produce some unusual wines – like their Blanc de Noirs from Shiraz and Muscat – and were the first to market a wine labelled 'Hárslevelü'. They have recently produced very acceptable Chardonnays at good prices.

ADDRESS: Van Loveren,
P. O. Box 19, Klaasvoogds 6707
TELEPHONE: (0234) 5 1505
FAX: (0234) 5 1336
WINE SALES AND TASTING:
Weekdays: 08h30 to 13h00 and
14h00 to 17h00
Saturdays: 09h30 to 13h00
Tastings are free of charge.
CELLAR TOURS: No cellar tours.
WINES:
Chardonnay ★★★★ The first release, the 1987, is very creditable for a first attempt. It has shown well at a number of tastings. The 1989 is consistently well rated in blind tastings, and makes big, soft, easy drinking. Cellar samples show a

very good 1990.
Gewürztraminer ★★★(★)
Noble Late Harvest ★★★(★)
Blanc de Blanc ★★★
Cape Riesling ★★★
Dry Red ★★★
Fernão Pires ★★★
Hárslevelü ★★★
Pinot Gris ★★★
Premier Grand Crû ★★★
Rhine Riesling ★★★
Riesling ★★★
Special Late Harvest ★★★
Blanc de Noir Muscat ★★(★)
Blanc de Noir Shiraz ★★
Colombar ★★
Late Vintage ★★
Sauvignon Blanc ★★

The large signboard outside the cellar at Van Loveren shows the way for prospective visitors.

WELTEVREDE

A few kilometres outside Bonnievale, on the road to Robertson, is Weltevrede which can be translated as 'well satisfied' – as the Jonkers, who have owned property here since 1912, should be. Weltevrede has been a leader in every respect. It was the first farm to register as an estate in the area and then to bottle and sell direct to the public. It was the first cellar to certify a Muscadel in South Africa and to wood mature white wines in the area, as well as being the first to put a wine onto the market from the locally bred grape, Therona. Now Lourens Jonker has produced a single-vineyard wine bottled under the label 'Oupa se Wingerd Red Muscadel'.

Weltevrede produces a wide range of wines, including excellent Chardonnays, Rhine Rieslings, Noble Late Harvests and, of course, superb fortified Muscats.

ADDRESS: Weltevrede Wine Estate,
P. O. Box 6, Bonnievale 6730
TELEPHONE: (02346) 2141/2/6
FAX: (02346) 2460
WINE SALES AND TASTING:
Weekdays: 08h30 to 13h00 and
14h00 to 17h00

Saturdays: 09h30 to 11h30
Tastings are free of charge.
CELLAR TOURS: Guided cellar tours are held by appointment.
WINES:
Muscat de Hambourg ★★★★ A beautiful, light, red dessert wine

with fine cultivar character. It regularly carries Superior certification.
Oupa se Wingerd Red Muscadel ★★★★ To my knowledge the only 'single vineyard' fortified wine in the Cape. The label honours Weltevrede's founder, Klaas Jonker. This is a deep, rich, red wine which was South African Champion Muscat at the national young wine show.
Colombard ★★★(★)
Noble Late Harvest ★★★(★)
Privé ★★★(★)

Special Late Harvest ★★★(★)
Blanc de Blanc ★★★
Blanc de Noir ★★★
Blanc Fumé ★★★
Cape Riesling ★★★
Gewürztraminer ★★★
Privé de Bois ★★★
Rhine Riesling ★★★
Rooi Muscadel ★★★
Sauvignon Blanc ★★★
Therona Late Harvest ★★★
Therona Special Late Harvest ★★★
Wit Muscadel ★★★
Chardonnay ★★
Late Vintage ★★

ZANDVLIET

Zandvliet Estate, situated in the Cogmanskloof near Ashton, is remarkable for the quality red wines it produces. Zandvliet Shiraz, originally launched in 1975, has proved that the area need not only produce white wines and Muscats. A Cabernet Sauvignon has also been recently introduced.

Apart from its wines, the estate is famous as a thoroughbred stud farm, and has bred horses such as Peter Beware, Caradoc, Smackeroo and Wild West.

ADDRESS: Zandvliet Estate,
P. O. Box 36, Ashton 6715
TELEPHONE: (0234) 5 1146
WINE SALES AND TASTINGS: The wines are marketed through the

Bergkelder, and so are not available for sale on the estate.
CELLAR TOURS: Guided cellar tours are held by appointment.

Swartland

The Swartland wine region lies on the west coast of the southwestern Cape, with the wine route stretching from Malmesbury in the south to Piketberg in the north. The name Swartland (black land) derives from the bush – known as Renosterbos ('Rhinoceros-bush') – which covers this area and appears black when wet. The land looks far from black in spring, however, when the wild flowers of the region bring a profusion of colour, enticing tourists from all over the country (an annual wild-flower show takes place every September in Darling). The cellars of the wine route are all quite close to the west-coast holiday-making places like Langebaan and Saldanha. The waters of this coast, provide a wealth of seafood, including crayfish, oysters and perlemoen.

Bird life has always been an attraction of the area, and with the creation of the National Park at Langebaan – to add to the birding attractions of Langebaan lagoon and the port at Saldanha – it is sure to improve. Nowadays the Swartland is also the home of a traditional-Italian-cheese-making operation, La Cima just outside Malmesbury. Those who wish to sample the Pecorino, Ricotta, Provolone and other cheeses produced can phone Mrs Ciman (Tel. (0224) 77024). The area is also deservedly well known for its fine wheat and sheep farms, as well as for its hospitable people.

If you wish to stay in the area, you could take advantage of this hospitality and stay at one of the many private farms that offer accommodation – phone Kontrei Farm Holidays (021) 96 0146.

ALLESVERLOREN

The first wines on this historical estate – owned by the Malan family since 1870 – were planted in 1780. Its wines, especially Shiraz and Port, have won many local and international awards. The Port has long been considered one of the best in the country.

ADDRESS: Allesverloren Estate, P. O. Box 23, Riebeeck-Wes 6800
TELEPHONE: (02246) 320
WINE SALES AND TASTING: Wines are marketed by the Bergkelder, so no wine is sold from the estate. Tastings are held by appointment.
CELLAR TOURS: Guided cellar tours are held by appointment.

MAMREWEG CO-OPERATIVE

Approximately 30 kilometres from Malmesbury on the R315 to Darling is the Mamreweg Co-op. Founded in 1949, the cellar has a reputation for good Cinsaut, and favourably priced wines. This is a wonderful area to visit in the height of the wild-flower season.

ADDRESS: Mamreweg Co-op, P. O. Box 114, Darling 7345 (address enquiries to the Public Relations Officer)
TELEPHONE: (02241) 2276/7
WINE SALES AND TASTING: Sales Mondays to Thursdays: 08h00 to 17h30
Fridays: 08h00 to 16h00
Saturdays: 09h00 to 12h00
Tastings by appointment (for groups).
CELLAR TOURS: Guided cellar tours by appointment (for groups).

WINES:
Cinsaut ★★★
Special Late Harvest ★★(★)
Blanc de Blanc ★★
Chenin Blanc ★★
Colombar ★★
Dry Steen ★★
Grand Crû ★★
Hanepoot ★★
Late Harvest ★★
Pinotage ★★
Tinta Barocca ★★
Blanc de Noir ★(★)
Stein ★
Claret (no rating)

PORTERVILLE CO-OPERATIVE

Almost 60 per cent of the wine from this co-op – which was founded in 1941 – is made from Steen and Colombar. The cellar draws its grapes from over 130 members, and most of the wine produced is sold in bulk, only a small amount being bottled for sale from the cellar.

ADDRESS: Porterville Co-op, P. O. Box 52, Porterville 6810
TELEPHONE: (02623) 2170
WINE SALES AND TASTING:
Weekdays: 08h00 to 13h00 and 14h00 to 17h00
Saturdays: 08h00 to 11h00
Tastings are free of charge.
CELLAR TOURS: Guided cellar tours are held on request.
WINES:
Pinotage ★★
Premier Grand Crû ★★
Blanc de Blanc ★
Golden Hanepoot Jerepigo ★
Late Vintage ★
Sauvignon Blanc (no rating)

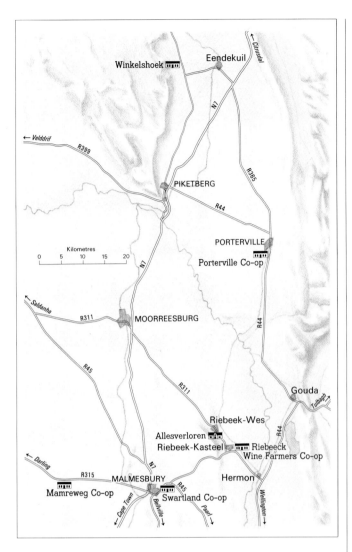

RIEBEEK WINE FARMERS CO-OPERATIVE

This co-operative was founded in 1941, to service some of the oldest wine farms in the country scattered around the historic Kasteelberg near the towns of Riebeek-Wes and Riebeek-Kasteel.

ADDRESS: Riebeek Wine Farmers' Co-op, P. O. Box 13, Riebeek-Kasteel 6801
TELEPHONE: (02244) 63 8386/ 63 8504
WINE SALES AND TASTING: Weekdays: 08h30 to 12h30 and 13h30 to 17h30
Saturdays: 08h30 to 12h00
Tastings are held by appointment for large groups.
CELLAR TOURS: Guided cellar tours are held by appointment for large groups.

WINES:
Special Late Harvest ★★★(★)
Blanc de Noir ★★★
Chenin Blanc ★★★
Late Harvest ★★★
Port ★★★
Shiraz ★★(★)
Weisser Riesling ★★(★)
Cabernet Sauvignon ★★
Colombard ★★
Fortified Muscat Wines ★★
Pinotage ★★
Premier Grand Crû ★★
Riesling ★★

SWARTLAND CO-OPERATIVE

This large co-op, founded in April 1948 by a group of 15 farmers, is five kilometres from Malmesbury, in the heart of the Swartland. It is the largest co-operative operation to sell all its wine in bottle in the country. Swartland has a consistently good show record, and is well known for its Pinotage and Tinta Barocca. The co-op is very active in its marketing efforts.

ADDRESS: Swartland Co-op, P. O. Box 95, Malmesbury 7300
TELEPHONE: (0224) 2 1434/1134/1135
WINE SALES AND TASTING: Sales Weekdays: 08h30 to 13h00 and 14h00 to 17h00
Saturdays: 09h00 to 12h00
Tastings are free of charge.
Weekdays: 08h30 to 13h00 and 14h00 to 16h30
Saturdays: 09h00 to 12h00
CELLAR TOURS: Guided cellar tours are held at 11h00 and 15h00.
WINES:
Pinotage ★★★(★)
Cuvée Brut ★★★
Hanepoot ★★★
Rooi Jerepiko ★★★
Sauvignon Blanc ★★★
Steen ★★★
Blanc de Noir ★★(★)
Demi Sec ★★(★)

Port ★★(★)
Blanc de Blanc ★★
Bukettraube ★★
Cabernet Sauvignon ★★
Chenin Blanc ★★
Cinsaut ★★
Colombar ★★
Dry Red ★★
Fernão Pires ★★
Furmint ★★
Hársevelü ★★
Premier Grand Crû ★★
Riesling ★★
Shiraz ★★
Special Late Harvest ★★
Stein ★★
Tinta Barocca ★★
White Jerepiko ★★
Late Vintage ★
Colombar Semi-dry (no rating)
Nouveau (no rating)
Rosé (no rating)

WINKELSHOEK

Twenty-eight kilometres north of Piketberg, on the road to Elandsbaai (the 'Kreef route'), is this cellar owned by the Hanekoms. It is near the Eendekuil cheese factory, and known for its Jerepigo and brandies.

ADDRESS: Winkelshoek Wine Cellar, P. O. Box 2, Eendekuil 7335
TELEPHONE: (02624) 830
FAX: (02624) 678
WINE SALES AND TASTING: Weekdays: 09h00 to 12h00 and 14h00 to 19h00

Saturdays: 09h00 to 12h00
There are no tastings (though plans are underway to introduce them).
CELLAR TOURS: No cellar tours (these too are planned for the future).

Vines near Riebeeck-Kasteel grow alongside wheat – the Swartland's major crop.

Olifants River

The Olifants River Wine Trust was established in 1986, and stretches from Citrusdal in the south to Lutzville in the north – some 150 kilometres along the river valley. Not all the wineries on the wine route are situated near the river, however, so a complete route could involve travelling over 200 kilometres, depending on which route you take. The route covers a considerable variation of terrain, the Cederberg, the Olifants River valley, and semi-desert regions (the Knersvlakte) – even the sea of the west coast is not far off. The best way to tackle this route – if you want to make a comprehensive job of it – is to allow yourself a few days, base yourself in Clanwilliam, and set out in different directions each morning.

Wine making in the area dates back to the 18th century, when the first white settlers arrived here. In fact, in 1815, a fortified sweet wine from the farm Brak-fontein near Citrusdal was supplied to Napoleon during his exile on St Helena.

As with the Swartland, wild flowers are a feature of this area in spring, and are a major tourist attraction. The coast offers all the best seafood from the cold Atlantic at places like Lamberts Bay, Elands Bay and Doring Bay. Organized tours of the area include crayfish-and-wine tours and flowers-and-wine tours. For further information on these, or anything else on this area, contact the Olifants River & West Coast Tourism Bureau (Tel. (02724) 6 1731/3).

CEDERBERG CELLARS

It is worth the 50-odd-kilometre drive off the N7 into the Cederberg and through the Algeria camping grounds to visit this mountain winery operated by Flippie Nieuwoudt. At an altitude of over 1100 metres this ranks as the highest winery in the Cape.

ADDRESS: Cederberg Kelders, Dwarsrivier, P. O. Box Cederberg, Clanwilliam 8136
TELEPHONE: (02682) ask for 1531/1521
WINE SALES AND TASTING:
Weekdays: 08h30 to 17h00
Saturdays: 08h30 to 12h00
Tastings are free of charge.
CELLAR TOURS: There are no cellar tours.
WINES:
Blanc de Noir ★★★
Cabernet Sauvignon ★★★
Sauvignon Blanc ★★★
Bukettraube ★★(★)
Dwarsrivier Wiessberger ★★(★)
Chenin Blanc ★★
Pinotage ★★
Cape Riesling ★(★)

CITRUSDAL CO-OPERATIVE

If ever a cellar has made an effort to improve its products and their packs it has been Citrusdal Co-op, producer of Goue Vallei wines. This large Co-op crushes over 8 000 tons from some 120 members. The attractive Goue Vallei wines had daisies on the labels in 1989, and proteas of the Cederberg in 1990. Part of the revenue generated by the sale of these wines is donated to the Ramskop Nature Reserve in Clanwilliam. The Goue Vallei range is excellent value for money.

ADDRESS: Citrusdal Co-op, P. O. Box 41, Citrusdal 7340
TELEPHONE: (02662) ask for 94/121
WINE SALES AND TASTING:
Sales Weekdays: 08h00 to 12h30 and 14h00 to 17h00
Saturdays: 08h30 to 12h30
Wine may be tasted: tastings are free of charge.
CELLAR TOURS: Guided cellar tours are held on request during the week. Large groups should book.

WINES:
Blanc de Blanc ★★★
Hárslevelü ★★(★)
Bukettraube ★★
Chenin Blanc ★★
Dal Rouge ★★

KLAWER CO-OPERATIVE

Klawer is the Cape's third-largest cellar, and crushes over 25 000 tons of grapes a year. It is situated three kilometres from the town of the same name, and boasts attractive sales and tasting facilities. In 1985, the co-op's Colombar won a gold medal at the International Wine and Spirit Competition in Britain.

ADDRESS: Klawer Co-op, P. O. Box 8, Klawer 8145
TELEPHONE: (02724) 6 1530
WINE SALES AND TASTING:
Weekdays: 08h00 to 17h00
CELLAR TOURS: Cellar tours are held on request.
RESTAURANT: Meals can be arranged for groups by appointment.
WINES:
Red Muscadel ★★★
Soet Hanepoot ★★★
Soet Wit Muscadel ★★★
Vonkelwyn Demi Sec ★★(★)
Blanc de Noir ★★
Chenin Blanc ★★
Hárslevelü ★★
Premier Grand Crû ★★
Sauvignon Blanc ★★
Shiraz ★★
Special Late Vintage ★★
Vonkelwyn Sec ★★
Late Vintage ★
Pinotage ★
Colombar (no rating)
Port (no rating)
Stein (no rating)

LUTZVILLE CO-OPERATIVE

This co-op just outside Lutzville crushes nearly 30 000 tons of grapes a year. A lot of the vineyards supplying the co-op are close to the sea (15 kilometres away) and are thus surprisingly cool.

The co-op makes a real effort to keep the price of their wines within the reach of consumers.

ADDRESS: Lutzville Co-op, P. O. Box 50, Lutzville 8165
TELEPHONE: (02725) 7 1516
WINE SALES AND TASTING:
Weekdays: 08h00 to 12h30 and 14h00 to 17h00
Saturdays: 08h30 to 12h00
Tastings are free of charge.
CELLAR TOURS: Guided cellar tours are held by appointment.
WINES:
Chenin Blanc ★★
Fleermuisklip Emerald Riesling ★★
Fleermuisklip Sauvignon Blanc ★★
Blanc de Noir ★
Bukettraube ★
Hanepoot ★
Laatoes ★

SPRUITDRIFT CO-OPERATIVE

Spruitdrift is another of the giant cellars of the Olifants River region, crushing between 22 000 and 24 000 tons of grapes annually and making a wide range of types and styles of wine. The co-op is progressive in its thinking, and makes use of screw-top bottles to try to keep the cost of their wine down as far as possible. Spruitdrift has produced the area's first Gewürztraminer, and will soon have a Cabernet available.

ADDRESS: Spruitdrift Co-op, P. O. Box 129, Vredendal 8160
TELEPHONE: (0271) 3 3086/7
WINE SALES AND TASTING:
Weekdays: 08h00 to 17h30
Saturdays: 08h00 to 12h00
Tastings are free of charge.
CELLAR TOURS: Guided cellar tours

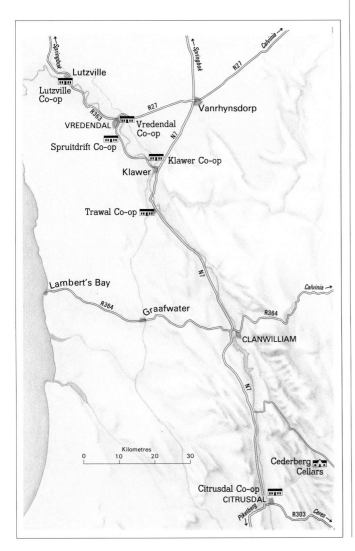

The Clanwilliam Dam on the Olifants River lies to the west of the Cederberg mountain range.

are organized as required. Best to phone in advance, especially groups.
WINES:
Muskadel Jerepiko ★★★(★)
Special Late Harvest ★★★(★)
Sweet Hanepoot ★★★(★)
Chenin Blanc ★★★
Late Harvest ★★★
Port ★★★
Pinotage ★★(★)
Blanc de Noir ★★
Dry Red ★★
Premier Grand Crû ★★
Sauvignon Blanc ★★
Rosé ★
Colombar (no rating)

TRAWAL CO-OPERATIVE

This co-operative cellar is 12 kilometres beyond Klawer, and is the only cellar in the area that does not bottle any of its wine – their wines are supplied to merchants in bulk.

ADDRESS: Trawal Wynkelders, P. O. Box 2, Klawer 8145
TELEPHONE: (02724) 6 1616
WINE SALES AND TASTING: No wine sales or tasting.
CELLAR TOURS: Guided cellar tours are held by appointment.

VREDENDAL CO-OPERATIVE

Pressing almost 50 000 tons of grapes a year makes this South Africa's largest cellar. To manage such an operation takes a special kind of person and this comes in the form of genial giant, Gielie Swiegers. Probably the Cape's highest-paid wine maker, Gielie is also one of the most innovative. His labels are leaders in style, and ideas for launches match the very best.

ADDRESS: Vredendal Co-op, P. O. Box 75, Vredendal 8160
TELEPHONE: (0271) 3 1080
WINE SALES AND TASTING:
Weekdays: 08h00 to 12h30 and 14h00 to 17h30
Saturdays: 08h00 to 12h00
Tastings are free of charge.
CELLAR TOURS: Guided cellar tours are held on weekdays at 10h00 and 15h00.
WINES:
Hanepoot Jerepigo ★★★★ This is a traditional full-flavoured Muscat.
Red Jerepigo ★★★(★)
Fernão Pires ★★★
Koekenaap Chardonnay ★★★
Muscadel Jerepigo ★★★
Port ★★★
Sauvignon Blanc ★★★
Bukettraube ★★(★)
Hárslevelü ★★(★)
Late Harvest ★★(★)
Grand Crû ★★
Pinotage ★★
Special Late Harvest ★★
Chenin Blanc ★
Goiya Kgeisje (no rating)
Vredendaal Vonkelwyn (no rating)

Klein Karoo

This route developed out of the tiny Calitzdorp Wine Route, which now operates within the Klein Karoo Wine Route, but still retains its original logo. The Calitzdorp route began in 1984, with Carel Nel of Boplaas being the driving force behind its establishment. The Klein Karoo Route was developed in 1986.

As you travel the R62 northeast from Ashton towards Montagu you enter the Klein Karoo through Thomas Bain's Tunnel in Cogmanskloof. Montagu is traditionally Muscadel country. However, as you continue along the R62 through Barrydale and Calitzdorp to Oudtshoorn and surrounds you will find some good natural wines and stunning ports in the Portuguese style.

The size of the Klein Karoo Wine Route (i.e. the distances that have to be travelled) limits the choice of wineries that it is possible to visit in a day, so it is a good idea to make a decision on which ones you are interested in before you decide where to base yourself. Probably the best place to stay from the point of view of doing the wine route is George (for information on accommodation phone the Satour Visitors' Information Bureau – Tel. (0441) 5228) – from where you can visit the wineries of Oudtshoorn, De Rust and Calitzdorp. It is possible to cover the same area while stationed at Oudtshoorn (Oudtshoorn Municipal Publicity Office Tel. (04431) 2221) – which also has the interesting diversions of the Kango Caves and ostrich farms to offer.

To visit the wineries at the western end of the wine route, you should stay at Montagu (Montagu Tourism Information Bureau, Tel. (0234) 4 2471) – either at one of the hotels, or at the delightful Mimosa Lodge, which boasts superb cuisine (Tel. (0234) 4 2351).

BARRYDALE CO-OPERATIVE WINERY AND DISTILLERY

Wine making has always been more of a sideline at this co-op, which has, until recently, concentrated on making brandy. This still happens, but in recent years more attention has been given to production of quality wine. Situated at the western entrance of the attractive town that it takes its name from, the co-op was established in 1940, and today is the only co-op that produces brandy in the Cape.

ADDRESS: Barrydale Co-op,
P. O. Box 59, Barrydale 6750
TELEPHONE: (02971) ask for 12
WINE SALES AND TASTING:
Weekdays: 08h30 to 12h30 and
13h30 to 17h00
Saturdays (December to January):
09h00 to 12h30
Tastings are free of charge.
CELLAR TOURS: Guided cellar tours
are held on request.
WINES:
Chardonnay ★★★(★)
Special Late Harvest ★★★

Blanc de Noir ★★
Demi-Sec Sparkling Wine ★★
Red Muscadel ★★
Sauvignon Blanc ★★
Sparkling Wine Dry ★★
White Muscadel ★★
Blanc de Blanc ★
Chenel ★
Chenin Blanc ★
Colombar ★
Blanc Fumé (no rating)
Muscat d'Alexandrie Jerepigo (no rating)
Riesling (no rating)

BOPLAAS

The Nels of Boplaas are pioneers by any standards. Eager to explore, discover, and improve upon whatever they undertake. Boplaas' cellars and homesteads lie on the edge of the village of Calitzdorp, and are easily found by following the striking Calitzdorp Wine Route signs. The vineyards then spread out from the cellars across the valley and onto the hill-slopes. The attractive sales area is built in the style of some 200 years ago with poplar beams and a riet ceiling. Here can also be seen Carel Nel's collection of Stone Age implements.

The Nels are long-established Karoo people and have records showing exports of Brandy to London back in 1850. Their modern wine-making dates back to 1979 when extensive replanting with classic cultivars began. Much experimental and developmental work has been done since then, and they are leaders in the Karoo wine-producing industry, with red cultivars like Cabernet Sauvignon, Merlot, and Cabernet Franc, as well as whites by way of Sauvignon Blanc and Weisser Riesling. Their most outstanding wines, however, are their Ports, made in true Portuguese style and using a range of traditional Port varieties. Boplaas Ports have been South Africa's champions on a number of occasions.

Boplaas also own Southern Cellars, a wholesale operation where they search for great examples of dessert wines to bottle under the Southern Cellars label, which shows a rare protea discovered in the Calitzdorp mountains, the Golden Mimetes. They have also developed Ruiterbosch Mountain Vineyards (see page 75) on the Outeniqua Mountains overlooking Mossel Bay, from which they have so far produced Weisser Riesling and Sauvignon Blanc.

ADDRESS: Boplaas Estate,
P. O. Box 156, Calitzdorp 6660
TELEPHONE: (04437) 3 3326
FAX: (04437) 3 3750
WINE SALES AND TASTING:
Weekdays: 08h00 to 13h00 and
14h00 to 17h00
Saturdays: 09h00 to 12h00
Tastings are free of charge.

CELLAR TOURS: Guided cellar tours
are available on request.
RESTAURANT: From 5 December to
10 January, and for two weeks
over the Easter holidays,
home-cooked farm lunches are
served between 12h00 and 14h00
in the sales area or on the lawns
outside (adults: R15-00 plus tax,

The Swartberg Pass, built by Thomas Bain between 1881 and 1888, cuts through the Swartberg mountains near Prince Albert, on the way to Oudtshoorn.

children under 12: R9-00 plus tax).
WINES:
Vintage Reserve Port ★★★★(★)
This cellar has produced excellent Ports over a number of years and, after a good run of medals and awards, achieved South African Champion status in 1986. The flagship wine comes from selected barrels and is now bottled with a distinctly 'Portuguese-style' label in an imported Portuguese Port bottle. It is only available from the estate. The 1989 is the best ever, and is the first Port to which I have given five stars. Sales are limited to six bottles per person at R23-00 each.
Grand Vin Rouge ★★★★ A very limited quantity (120 cases) was made available in mid-1990. The 90 per cent Cabernet and 10 per cent Merlot give a very attractive fruity nose and good concentrated, elegant flavours backed by fine oak.
Muscadel ★★★★ This Wine of Origin Klein Karoo is a deep-yellow, full-bodied, sweet wine with lots of intense good Muscadel character. The 1988 is splendid.
Red Dessert ★★★★ The first release of this lovely wine was from the 1987 vintage and was made from Tinta Barocca. The 1988 is very Port-like and makes delicious sipping.
Vintage Port ★★★★ This Port is sold with the traditional Boplaas label. It has the Boplaas pedigree of awards behind it. The 1988 has been bottled at under two years of age and so will benefit from long ageing (ten years or more) in the bottle. This product's label will also become more 'Portuguese' with the 1989 bottling.
Cabernet ★★★(★)
Merlot ★★★(★)
Blanc de Noir ★★★
Pinot Noir Sparkling Wine ★★★
Ruby Port ★★★
Sauvignon Blanc ★★★
Special Late Harvest ★★★
White Port ★★★
Late Harvest ★★(★)
Tinta Barocca ★★(★)
Blanc Fumé ★★
Dry Red ★★
Sauvignon Blanc Light ★★
Sparkling Wine (Sweet) ★★
Sweet Hanepoot ★★
Vin Blanc ★★
Hanepoot (no rating)
Red Jerepiko (no rating)

CALITZDORP CO-OPERATIVE

This winery was established way back in 1928 by a group of 15 farmers as the Calitzdorp Fruit Exporters Co-operative. The co-op has over 100 members scattered over a large area stretching from the Swartberg mountains to the sea, and delivering over 3 000 tons of grapes annually. Wine production began during the Second World War, and the co-op specializes in dessert wines. Their wines are sold under the Buffelskroon label.

ADDRESS: Calitzdorp Co-op,
P. O. Box 193, Calitzdorp 6660
TELEPHONE: (04437) 3 3328/01
WINE SALES AND TASTING:
Weekdays: 08h00 to 12h15 and 13h15 to 17h00
Saturdays: 08h00 to 12h00
Wine may be tasted: tastings are free of charge.
CELLAR TOURS: There are no cellar tours available.

WINES:
Hanepoot ★★
Muskadel ★★
Semi-sweet Red ★★
Semi-sweet White Table Wine ★★
Tinta Barocca ★★
Buffelskroon Blanc de Noir ★
Buffelskroon Pinotage ★
Port ★
Sauvignon Blanc (no rating)
Vin Rosetta (no rating)

DIE KRANS

Die Krans is right next door to Boplaas, and in fact was once part of a larger property owned by Chris and Danie Nel who amicably agreed to divide the property in 1980.

Die Krans is now operated by the brothers Boets and Strobel, who have undertaken a major move to grow varieties like Cabernet and Chardonnay on the higher slopes of the surrounding mountains. Dessert wines are still their main business, though, and they donate a portion of the proceeds of one of them, 'La Difference', to the Kanga Mountain Reserve to help preserve the Cape Mountain Zebra.

ADDRESS: Die Krans Estate,
P. O. Box 28, Calitzdorp 6660
TELEPHONE: (04437) 3 3314
WINE SALES AND TASTINGS:
Weekdays: 08h00 to 17h00
Saturdays: 09h00 to 12h30
Tastings are free of charge.
CELLAR TOURS: Guided cellar tours are held hourly from 08h00 during December and January, and for two weeks over Easter – or on request during the rest of the year.
RESTAURANT: During December and January, and for two weeks over Easter, cheese lunches (R15-00 a head) are served between 12h00 and 14h00 Monday to Saturday. At other times of the year they can be arranged by appointment for groups of more than 10 people.
TOURS: A 25-minute, self-guided

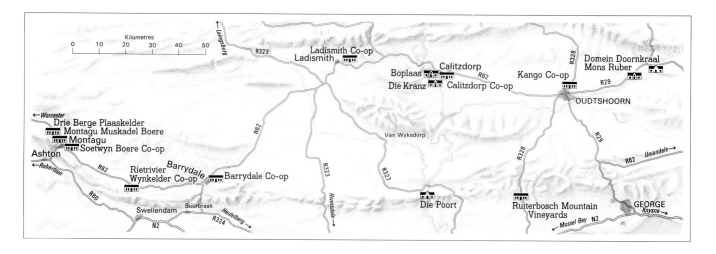

vineyard trail is offered, beginning at the wine tasting centre. It meanders through the vineyards and signs tell you what cultivars you are walking past. An easy stroll brings you back to the tasting room.
WINES:
Muscat d'Alexandrie ★★★(★)
Noble Late Harvest ★★★(★)
Port ★★★(★)
L'Enchenté ★★★
Shiraz ★★★

Special Late Harvest ★★★
White Muskadel Jerepigo ★★★
Blanc de Noir ★★(★)
Chenin Blanc ★★(★)
Late Harvest ★★(★)
Tinta Barocca ★★(★)
Fernâo Pires ★★
Gewürztraminer ★★
Hárslevelü ★★
Pinotage ★★
Droë Rooiwyn ★
La Difference (no rating)

DOMEIN DOORNKRAAL

On the road from Oudtshoorn to De Rust (R29), on the left hand side (three kilometres west of Le Roux station) is the colourful outlet for Domein Doornkraal. Swepie le Roux is one of the more eccentric wine producers of the Cape, and humorous names and labels are a feature of his wines.

ADDRESS: Domein Doornkraal,
P. O. Box 104, De Rust 6650
TELEPHONE: (04439) 6715/2551
WINE SALES AND TASTING:
Weekdays: 09h00 to 17h00 outside school holidays, 08h00 to 18h00 during school holidays
Saturdays: 09h00 to 15h00
Wine may be tasted: tastings are free of charge.
CELLAR TOURS: Guided cellar tours are held in request.

WINES:
Hanepoot ★★★
Kaptein ★★★
Pinta ★★★
Tickled Pink ★★★
Kuierwyn ★★(★)
Muscadel ★★(★)
Port ★★
Serenade (Dry) ★★
Serenade (Semi-sweet) ★★
Tinta Bianca ★★
Majoor ★(★)

DRIE BERGE PLAASKELDER

Drie Berge is on the scenic road from Montagu to Koo Drie Berge Cellars. They have their own range of wines for sale.

ADDRESS: Drie Berge Plaaskelder,
P. O. Box 37, Montagu 6720
TELEPHONE: (0234) 4 1305
WINE SALES AND TASTING:
Weekdays: 09h00 to 12h30 and

13h30 to 18h00
Saturdays: 09h00 to 13h00
Tastings are free of charge.
CELLAR TOURS: Guided cellar tours are available on request.

KANGO CO-OPERATIVE

Kango began life as a tobacco co-op in 1926. In 1974, it was expanded to make wine as well, and to take grapes previously delivered to Union Wine, who closed their Oudtshoorn production facilities that year. The 50 or so members deliver some 5 000 tons of grapes annually. A range of natural wines are produced under the Rijckshof label, but the dessert wines are consistently their better products. The co-op is located in the Oudtshoorn industrial area.

ADDRESS: Kango Co-op,
P. O. Box 46, Oudtshoorn 6620
TELEPHONE: (0443) 22 6065
WINE SALES AND TASTINGS:
Weekdays: 08h30 to 13h00 and 14h00 to 16h30
Tastings are free of charge.
CELLAR TOURS: Guided cellar tours are held by appointment.
WINES:
Golden Jerepiko ★★★★ A super fortified Steen and a regular award-winner. One of the best non-Muscat fortifieds.

Hanepoot ★★★
Red Muscadel ★★★
Rijckshof Chenin Blanc ★★★
White Muskadel ★★★
Rijckshof Claret ★★(★)
Special Late Harvest ★★(★)
Blanc de Noir ★★
Herfsgoud ★★
Hofheimer ★★
Port ★★
Red Jerepigo ★★
Rozelle ★★
Xandré ★★
Premier Blanc ★(★)

LADISMITH CO-OPERATIVE

As you enter Ladismith on the R62 from Barrydale, the co-op is on the right. Established in 1939, it now has some 120 members delivering almost 12 000 tons of grapes annually. Most of the production is distilled wine, but natural wine is playing an increasingly important role each year.

ADDRESS: Ladismith Co-op,
P. O. Box 56, Ladismith 6885
TELEPHONE: (02942) 31
WINE SALES AND TASTING:
Weekdays: 08h00 to 13h00 and 14h00 to 17h00
Tastings are free of charge.

CELLAR TOURS: Guided cellar tours are held on request.
WINES:
Chenin Blanc ★★
Swartberg Aristaat ★★
Towerkop Stein ★
Towerkop Dry Red (no rating)

MONS RUBER

The name 'Mons Ruber' comes from the red hills which dominate the countryside here. The tasting room is a restored coaching inn of the late 19th century, and it has now been declared a National Monument. At Mons Ruber, you will find an interesting collection of ostrich-feather articles, paintings and photographs, including some of the Royal visit to the estate in 1947, when the now Queen Mother, clipped the feathers of an ostrich. There is also a restored, late-19th-century kitchen.

Brandy is produced here, and has been since 1850. Nowadays a range of unusual fortified wines are the main attractions, though, along with interesting red and rosé natural wines. The estate commenced bottling in 1985.

To find Mons Ruber, follow the R29 from Oudtshoorn to Beaufort West via Meiringspoort. Before you reach De Rust you will see the turn off to the right for Mons Ruber almost opposite Le Roux station. Sign boards at the wagon will direct you to the sales and tasting venue.

ADDRESS: Mons Ruber Estate, Private Bag X629, Oudtshoorn 6620
TELEPHONE: (04439) 6812
WINE SALES AND TASTING:
Weekdays: 08h30 to 17h00
Saturdays: 08h30 to 13h00
Wines may be tasted: tastings are free of charge.
CELLAR TOURS: There are no cellar tours available.

WINES:
Red Jerepigo ★★★(★)
Muscadel Jerepigo ★★★
Hanepoot Jerepigo ★★(★)
Bonitas ★★
Cabernet Sauvignon ★★
Conari ★★
Elegantia ★★
Regalis ★★
Vino ★

MONTAGU MUSKADEL BOERE

The cellar is in the town of Montagu. Established in 1941, it crushes over 11 000 tons of grapes annually, and produces some very good Muscadels. The cellar supplies mainly in bulk to merchants, though it does bottle some wines for sale under its own label.

ADDRESS: Montagu Muskadel Boere Co-op, P. O. Box 29, Montagu 6720
TELEPHONE: (0234) 4 1125
WINE SALES AND TASTING:
Weekdays: 08h30 to 12h30 and 13h30 to 17h00
There are no organized tastings, though people who wish to buy

may taste.
CELLAR TOURS: No cellar tours.
WINES:
Rooi Muskadel ★★★
Chenin Blanc ★★
Colombar ★
Sauvignon Blanc ★
Late Vintage (no rating)

RIETRIVIER WYNKELDER CO-OPERATIVE

Twenty kilometres east of Montagu, on the R62 towards Barrydale, is this relatively new cellar, established in 1966. Less than 5 000 tons of grapes are crushed annually, and those mainly for brandy production. A range of natural wines, and a Red Muscadel are bottled, however.

ADDRESS: Rietrivier Co-op, P. O. Box 144, Montagu 6720
TELEPHONE: (0234) 4 1705
WINE SALES AND TASTING:
Weekdays: 08h00 to 13h00 and 14h00 to 15h00
Wines may be tasted: tastings are free of charge.
CELLAR TOURS: Guided cellar tours are held on request.

WINES:
Blanc de Blanc ★★
Chenel ★★
Colombar ★★
Late Harvest ★★
Chenin Blanc ★
Grand Crû Noir ★
Hárslevelü (no rating)
Stein (no rating)
Red Muscadel (no rating)

RUITERBOSCH MOUNTAIN VINEYARDS

On the Indian Ocean side of the Robinson Pass, which carries the R328 from Oudtshoorn to Mossel Bay, are the three-year-old vineyards of the Cape's coolest wine area. This daring experiment of the Nels of

Boplaas has shown great promise from its earliest releases. The cold wet winters, hard gravelly soils, and long cool ripening time in summer are resulting in a very different style of wines – extending the choice available to South Africans.

ADDRESS: Ruiterbosch Mountain Vineyards, P. O. Box 156, Calitzdorp 6660
TELEPHONE: (04437) 3 3326
FAX: (04437) 3 3750
WINE SALES AND TASTING: All sales and tastings take place at Boplaas, where the wines are made.

WINES:
Rhine Riesling ★★★★ In its youth, the first release, from the 1989 vintage, is a stunning dry wine. It should age interestingly.
Sauvignon Blanc ★★★
Cuvée Premier Vin Blanc ★★★
Pinot Noir ★★★

SOETWYN BOERE CO-OPERATIVE

Established a year after its neighbour, Montagu Muskadel Boere, Soetwyn Boere is a much smaller, more personalized cellar, which was headed by Kenneth Knipe for a remarkable 37 years, until he was taken seriously ill in 1990.

Some natural wines are bottled, but the cellar's best wines are the fortified Muscadels and Hanepoots.

ADDRESS: Soetwyn Boere Co-op, P. O. Box 332, Montagu 6720
TELEPHONE: (0234) 4 1340
WINE SALES AND TASTING:
Weekdays: 08h00 to 12h30 and 13h30 to 17h00
Saturdays: 09h00 to 12h00
Tastings are free of charge.
CELLAR TOURS: Guided cellar tours are held on request.
WINES:
Red Muskadel ★★★

Hanepoot ★★
Stein ★★
White Muscadel ★★
Hárslevelü ★
Perlé Hopewell ★
Sauvignon Blanc ★
Vonkelwyn ★
Chenin Blanc (no rating)
Colombar (no rating)
Ordinance Late Harvest (no rating)
Premier Grand Crû (no rating)

> *The following winery is not part of the Klein Karoo Wine Route, but it can nonetheless be visited.*

DIE POORT

Die Poort does not form part of the Klein Karoo route but is close enough to visit while in this area. If you take the N2 from Cape Town, turn away from the sea towards the mountains at Albertinia, then follow the signs. If you take the N2 from Mossel Bay, on the other hand, turn right to Herbertsdale and then, 50 kilometres further on, just across the Gouritz River, is the remote cellar of Die Poort. Once there, you will see how aptly named the cellar is, lying as it does near the great Poort through which the Gouritz thundered in the flood which devastated Laingsburg in 1981.

ADDRESS: Die Poort, P. O. Box 45, Albertinia 6795
TELEPHONE: (02952) ask for 2030
WINE SALES AND TASTING:
Weekdays: 08h00 to 18h00
Saturdays: 08h00 to 13h00
(Preferable to phone in advance.)
Tastings are free of charge.
CELLAR TOURS: Guided cellar tours

are held on request during harvest time.
WINES:
Port ★★★
Fortified Muscat Wines ★★
Frölich Stein ★★
Rochelle Dry Red ★
Late Vintage (no rating)

Although 'discovered' by an exploratory group sent out by Jan van Riebeeck in February 1658, the valley now known as Tulbagh was only settled some 40 years later, in 1700. The village was laid out in 1795, and a magistrate appointed in 1804. The magisterial district was named Tulbagh, in honour of Ryk Tulbagh, a former governor of the Cape.

The town is famous for its Louis Thibault Drostdy, as well as for its recovery from the 1969 earthquake. The houses of Kerk Street, which were severely damaged in the disaster, have been completely restored, and today make up the largest single group of national monuments in South Africa. The drostdy acts as host to the Drostdy range of wines and the sherries of the area. The building opens Mondays to Saturdays, 10h00 to 17h00, and sherries can be tasted in the cool underground cellar.

The original KWV wine house 'Paddagang' is just off Kerk Street, and is open daily (09h00 to 17h00) for teas and lunch except on Mondays. The church from which Kerk Street gets its name is now a museum (open Mondays to Saturdays) well worth visiting.

DROSTDY CO-OPERATIVE

Opposite the Tulbagh Co-op cellar is the original Drostdy building, now restored after the earthquake by the Distillers Corporation.

ADDRESS: Drostdy Co-op,
P. O. Box 85, Tulbagh 6820
TELEPHONE: (0236) 30 1086
WINE SALES AND TASTING:
Weekdays: 08h00 to 12h00 and
13h30 to 17h00
Saturdays: 08h30 to 12h00
CELLAR TOURS: Guided cellar tours
are held at 11h00 and 15h00 on
weekdays.
WINES: Sherries (Oude Meester)
★★★★ The Drostdy sherries are all

Wines of Origin Tulbagh and are
certified Superior. The range is
Pale Dry, Medium and Full Cream.
Blanc de Noir (no rating)
Claret (no rating)
Grand Crû (no rating)
Hanepoot (no rating)
Jerepigo (no rating)
Late Harvest (no rating)
Port (no rating)
Riesling (no rating)
Steen (no rating)

KLOOFZICHT

The attractive farm Kloofzicht is the home of Tulbagh's amazing red wine, Alter Ego – without doubt the best wine to come out of the Tulbagh valley.

ADDRESS: Kloofzicht, P. O. Box
101, Tulbagh 6820
TELEPHONE: (0236) 30 0658
WINE SALES AND TASTING:
Weekdays 10h00 to 16h00
Weekends by appointment.
Tastings are free of charge.
CELLAR TOURS: Guided cellar tours
are held on request
OTHER FACILITIES: An art gallery
hosts both group exhibitions and
one man shows.
There is also a charming three-
bedroomed cottage (sleeping six)

with a fully equipped kitchen is
avaibable for hire.
WINES:
Alter Ego ★★★★ This Tulbagh
estate, with its five-hectare
vineyard, has produced its first
wine from the 1989 vintage. Deep
rich colour, full nose, great
concentrated fruit, and deep layers
of flavour backed by good French
oak. As good as it tastes now it will
well reward ageing another four to
six years. An amazing red wine for a
valley known for its whites.

LEMBERG

This tiny Tulbagh estate is owned by Jan and Janey Muller, and was purchased by them in 1978. The farm is named after the Ukrainian town from which Jan's maternal family emigrated to South Africa. Lemberg is only 13 hectares in extent, and about half of this area is planted with vines. The winery consists pretty much of a 'lean to' arrangement that houses a modern press, stainless-steel tanks etc.

ADDRESS: Lemberg Estate,
P. O. Box 108, Tulbagh 6820
TELEPHONE: (0236) 30 0659

WINE SALES AND TASTING: Strictly
by appointment.

MONTPELLIER

Montpellier boasts almost 150 years ownership by one family, and as long an association with wine. The Therons became disenchanted by the bureaucracy in control of the wine industry, though, and this saw Montpellier wines lose some of their earlier appeal. However, the new plantings and new wine maker of 1990 will see the cellar back at its best. Owned by Jan and Hendrik De Wet-Theron, this large estate of over 600 hectares has some 100 hectares or so devoted to vines.

ADDRESS: Montpellier Estate,
P. O. Box 24, Tulbagh 6820
TELEPHONE: (0236) 30 0723
WINE SALES AND TASTING:
Weekdays 09h00 to 12h30 and 13h30
to 17h00
Saturdays 09h00 to 12h00
Tastings are free of charge.
CELLAR TOURS: There are no

organized cellar tours, but people
may wander through the cellars.
WINES:
Special Late Harvest ★★★(★)
Huiswyn ★★★
Roter Traminer ★★★
Suzanne Gardé ★★(★)
Late Harvest ★★
Tuinwingerd ★★

THEUNISKRAAL

One of the oldest estates still in production, having begun bottling back in 1930, this was also one of the first farms to become involved in the Bergkelder estate scheme. The wines are made by Kobus Jordaan, while the vineyards are farmed by his brother, Rennie.

ADDRESS: Theuniskraal Estate,
P. O. Box 34, Tulbagh 6820
TELEPHONE: (0236) 30 0689

WINE SALES AND TASTING: Visits by
appointment only.

TULBAGH KO-OPERATIEWE WYNKELDER

This is one of the Cape's oldest co-ops, having been formed way back in 1906. Today the co-op bottles wines under its own label, also produces the Paddagang Vignerons wines.

ADDRESS: Tulbagh Co-op,
P. O. Box 85, Tulbagh 6820
TELEPHONE: (0236) 30 1001
WINE SALES AND TASTING:
Weekdays 08h30 to 12h30 and

13h30 to 17h15
Saturdays 08h30 to 12h00
Tastings are free of charge.
CELLAR TOURS: There are no cellar
tours.

The name Twee Jongegezellen (meaning 'two young bachelors') refers to two Dutch school friends who settled at the Cape and procured this farm.

WINES:
Claret (no rating)
Grand Crû (no rating)
Hanepoot (no rating)
Jerepigo (no rating)
Late Harvest (no rating)
Port (no rating)
Riesling (perlé) (no rating)
Riesling (dry) (no rating)
Sauvignon Blanc (no rating)

TWEE JONGEGEZELLEN

Twee Jongegezellen, famous for its night-time harvesting, is a large estate – with over 270 hectares under vine – and a model of modern farming. It has a long and interesting history dating back to 1710 when the first grant of land, which includes the present estate, was made by the Dutch East India Company to a Huguenot settler – he named his farm La Rhône. The Krones are responsible for the modern development of the estate and its current magnificent condition. Buildings, ancient and modern, are all kept in an excellent state of repair, and the neatly tended gardens, lawns and flowers seem almost to link with the vineyards. The entire estate has an air of timelessness where modern blends effortlessly with old. Twee Jongegezellen was originally a sherry cellar but N. C. Krone changed all that, and made TJ a respected brand, known throughout the country for its light and delicate natural wines. More recently the energetic and innovative son, Nicky Krone, has revamped the range into four main wines packaged in distinct bottles. These blends are from time to time supplemented by a Noble Late Harvest called Engeltjiepipi. The latest addition to Twee Jongegezellen has been a *méthode champenoise* cellar claimed by Nicky to be earthquake-proof.

ADDRESS: Twee Jongegezellen, P. O. Box 16, Tulbagh 6820
TELEPHONE: (0236) 30 0680

WINE SALES AND TASTING: Visits by special appointment only.

Overberg

This used to be the KWV district of Caledon, and includes Villiersdorp, Caledon, Riviersonderend, Bredasdorp, Botrivier and Walker Bay. Some of the Cape's most southerly vineyards are to be found in this the coolest of the wine growing areas – vines do not receive as many hours of sun as in other areas because of the proximity of the mountains. The mean annual rainfall of this region is high – some 750 millimetres – and because of the coolness of the climate, the grapes ripen late in the season.

HAMILTON RUSSELL VINEYARDS

Situated in the Hemel-en-Aarde valley, about eight kilometres from Hermanus, Hamilton Russell Vineyards is owned by Tim Hamilton Russell, head of the South African division of the world-wide advertising agency, J. Walter Thompson. Hamilton Russell wines are amongst the best in the Cape – their 1986 Pinot Noir won the 1989 Diners Club Award, with the 1987 coming second. Tim Hamilton Russell has been courageous in his endeavours to get the Wine and Spirit Board to be more reasonable in their regulations.

ADDRESS: Hamilton Russell Vineyards, Oude Hemel en Aarde, P. O. Box 158, Hermanus 7200
TELEPHONE: (0283) 2 3441/0
WINE SALES AND TASTING: Sales and tastings at the winery strictly by appointment. However, the cellar's wines can be bought and tasted at the Hamilton Russell tasting room in the Hermanus Market Square, behind the Burgundy Restaurant (weekdays 09h00 to 13h00 and 14h00 to 16h30; Saturdays 09h00 to 13h00). Tastings are free of charge.
CELLAR TOURS: No cellar tours.
WINES:
Pinot Noir ★★★★★ This wine was once labelled 'Grand Vin Noir'.

The 1987 looks great.
Chardonnay ★★★★(★) This used to be called 'Premier Vin Blanc', but is now certified as Chardonnay. The 1989 is great and will develop with benefit over six to eight years.
Sauvignon Blanc ★★★★ Originally called 'Grand Vin Blanc', this is now a good representative of a well-wooded Sauvignon Blanc. The 1988 reflects the vintage, yet it is still one of the best, with good fruit flavour, but no wood. The 1989 is a lovely wine, but not quite up to the standard of the 1988.
Grand Vin Blanc ★★★(★)
Hemel-en-Aarde Grand Crû Noir ★★★(★)
Premier Reserve ★★★(★)

The picturesque town of Hermanus is home to the Hamilton Russell tasting room.

HEMEL-EN-AARDE WINERY

This cellar, is run by wine maker Peter Finlayson. The winery's first wine was made in 1991 from grapes that were bought in.

ADDRESS: Hemel-en-Aarde Winery, P. O. Box 303, Hermanus 7200
TELEPHONE: (0283) 23515
WINE SALES AND TASTING: Weekdays 08h30 to 17h00
CELLAR TOURS: Guided tours of the winery's cellars are held on request.
WINES:
Blended Dry White (no rating)
Chardonnay (no rating)
Pinot Noir (no rating)
Sauvignon Blanc (no rating)

Wellington

The town of Wellington was founded in 1837. It was known then as Limietvallei (frontier valley) or Wagenmakersvallei (wagon makers' valley) – the latter because it was the centre of wagon-making for the farming community. The name Wellington was given to the settlement in 1838 by the then Governor of the Cape, Sir George Napier (after the Duke of Wellington – victor at Waterloo). The original town was laid out on the farm Champagne and this should have been a good pointer to its wine future.

The town is also famous as the headquarters of the Dried Fruit Board, and as a centre for fine brandies, vineyard nurseries, and leather tanning, as well as boasting the southern hemisphere's largest piano-building concern.

BOVLEI CO-OPERATIVE

This is one of the Cape's oldest co-ops, having been established – with government support – in 1907, and starting wine production the following year. It was originally known as the Boven Vallei Co-operative winery. The co-operative managed to survive the rigorous early years before the advent of the KWV and the ensuing legislation which stabilized the struggling co-operative movement, and today is one of the most modern and well-equipped cellars. It has an excellent sales and tasting venue, with a magnificent view of the Dutoitskloof and Hawekwa mountains. Situated in the foothills of these mountains, on the R303, it is at the start of the Bain's Kloof pass if you are heading towards the Breë River.

Until 1982, the wines were sold in bulk to merchants. Now a selection is bottled and sold under the cellar's own label.

ADDRESS: Bovlei Co-op, P. O. Box 82, Wellington 7655
TELEPHONE: (02211) 3 1567/64 1283
FAX: (02211) 2 1386
WINE SALES AND TASTING: Weekdays 08h30 to 12h30 and 13h30 to 17h30
Saturdays 08h30 to 12h30
Tastings are free of charge.
CELLAR TOURS: Guided cellar tours are held by appointment for groups.
WINES:
Cabernet Sauvignon ★★★
Pinotage ★★★
Soet Hanepoot ★★★
Grand Crû ★★(★)
Grand Rouge ★★(★)
Bukettraube ★★
Dry Sparkling Wine ★★
Riesling ★★
Shiraz ★★
Special Late Harvest ★★
Stein ★★
Sauvignon Blanc ★(★)
Semi-sweet Sparkling Wine ★
Carignan (no rating)
Colombard (no rating)
Soet Rooihanepoot (no rating)

ONVERWACHT

The first and, at present, only wine estate in Wellington, Onverwacht is close to the centre of the town. Trevor Harris, a Cape Town business man, bought the farm in 1986, and the first wines were bottled in 1989. Each vintage has seen an improvement in quality.

ADDRESS: Onverwacht Estate, P. O. Box 438, Wellington 7655
TELEPHONE: (02211) 3 4315
WINE SALES AND TASTING: Weekdays 09h00 to 17h00
Tastings are free of charge.
CELLAR TOURS: Guided cellar tours are available for large groups by appointment.
WINES:
Savoire Brut ★★(★)
Tinta Barocca ★★(★)
Chenin Blanc ★★
Pétillant Rosé ★★
Weisser Riesling ★★

WAMAKERS VALLEI CO-OPERATIVE

A little younger than its neighbour, Wellington Wynboere, this co-op was founded in 1941, and has much the same sized membership, while crushing a slightly larger quantity of grapes. The name Wamakersvallei is a Dutch translation of 'Val du Charron', an appellation given to the area by the French Huguenots in 1688.

ADDRESS: Wamakers Vallei Co-op, P. O. Box 509, Wellington 7657
TELEPHONE: (02211) 3 1582
WINE SALES AND TASTING: Weekdays 08h00 to 12h30 and 14h00 to 17h00
Tastings are free of charge.
CELLAR TOURS: There are no cellar tours available.

WINES:
Premier Grand Crû ★★★
Cinsaut ★★
Hanepoort Jerepigo ★★
Pinotage ★★
Stein ★
Late Vintage (no rating)
Riesling (no rating)
Special Late Harvest (no rating)

WELLINGTON WYNBOERE CO-OPERATIVE

This is an old co-op, established in 1936, with about 45 members supplying in the region of 10 000 tons of grapes annually.

ADDRESS: Wellington Wynboere Co-op, P. O. Box 520, Wellington 7657
TELEPHONE: (02211) 3 1163
WINE SALES AND TASTING: Mondays to Fridays 08h00 to 12h30 and 14h00 to 17h00
Tastings are free of charge.
CELLAR TOURS: There are no cellar tours.

WINES:
Chenin Blanc ★★
Cinsaut ★★
Hanepoot Jerepigo ★★
Laatoes ★★
Riesling ★★
Stein ★★
Cabernet ★
Grand Crû (no rating)
Spesiale Laatoes (no rating)

Durbanville

Durbanville might not boast many wineries, but it has some of the finest wine-growing ground in the Cape. Close to the cool Atlantic Ocean, the deep, well-drained, mainly Hutton and Clovelly soils grow some of the finest grapes that appear in wines made in Stellenbosch. At the moment there are only four producing wineries in this area, which is rapidly losing its agricultural ground to the expanding city. The Durbanville Wine Trust will ensure that there is continuity in wine production in the area.

ALTYDGEDACHT

This estate is owned by the Parker family, and for years the wine was made by Mrs Jean Parker. Nowadays, son Oliver makes innovative wines while his brother John tends the vineyards.

ADDRESS: Altydgedacht Estate, P. O. Box 213, Durbanville 7550
TELEPHONE: (021) 96 1295
WINE SALES AND TASTING: Open for sales and tastings between September and April on Wednesdays 12h00 to 18h00 and Saturdays 09h00 to 12h00. Outside these times and dates only by appointment. Tastings are free of charge.
CELLAR TOURS: No cellar tours.
WINES:
Tintoretto ★★★★ The 1981 was a most unusual deep-flavoured wine, the good fruit and meaty flavours of which are due to its equal quantities of Barbera and Shiraz grapes. This is a wine that, as attractive as it is when young, has definitely benefited with time in the bottle, and is currently drinking very well. The next release is from the 1986 vintage and is a blend of 75 per cent Shiraz and 25 per cent Barbera. Don't be fooled by the wine's lightish colour, or pass it off as an insignificant wine – it isn't.
Cabernet Sauvignon ★★★(★)
Bukettraube ★★★
Chardonnay ★★★
Gewürztraminer ★★★
Pinotage ★★★
Sauvignon Blanc ★★★
Shiraz ★★★
Tygerberg Wood-aged White ★★★

BLOEMENDAL

Bloemendal, situated just beyond Altydgedacht, only began bottling wine in 1987, but grapes have been grown here for many years. Young Jackie Coetzee is the Elsenberg-trained wine maker producing most attractive wines with equally attractive labels.

ADDRESS: Bloemendal Estate, P. O. Box 466 Durbanville 7550
TELEPHONE: (021) 96 2682
WINE SALES AND TASTING: Sales Wednesdays 13h00 to 18h00
Saturdays 09h00 to 12h00
Tastings are held on appointment.
CELLAR TOURS: Guided tours of the estate's cellars are available on request.

WINES:
Cabernet Sauvignon ★★★★ The first release was from the 1987 vintage, which was launched in 1990. It is an elegant, fruity wine, full of berry character, good tannin and nice oaky background.
Bloemen Blanc ★★★(★)
Chardonnay ★★★
Sauvignon Blanc ★★★

DIEMERSDAL

For many years Diemersdal grew grapes for the KWV and participated in the KWV experimental vineyard schemes, so it always had unusual and new varieties. A very small proportion of their wine has appeared under KWV labels for members only. Nineteen ninety one sees the launch of wine maker, Tienie Louw's first wines to the public.

ADDRESS: Diemersdal Estate, P. O. Box 23, Durbanville 7550
TELEPHONE: (021) 96 3361
WINE SALES AND TASTING: Sales Wednesdays 13h00 to 18h00 Saturdays 09h00 to 16h00
Wine tastings by appointment.
CELLAR TOURS: Guided cellar tours are held by appointment only.
WINES:
Diemersdal ★★★(★)
Diemersdal Cabernet ★★★

MEERENDAL

This was the first estate in the Durbanville area to produce wine under its own label. Meerendal, which has been producing wines since 1716, is now owned by the Starke family, and third generation William has recently joined Kosie as wine maker. They are known for their superb Pinotage and Shiraz wines – and have a Merlot still to come – but also grow fine white varieties for the Bergkelder through whom their wines are marketed.

ADDRESS: Meerendal Estate, P. O. Box 2, Durbanville 7550
TELEPHONE: (021) 96 1915
WINE SALES AND TASTING: No wine sales, visits by appointment only.

Index

Aan de Doorns Co-operative	56	Dieu Donné	54	L'Ormarins	55	Ruiterbosch Mountain	
Agterkliphoogte Co-operative	62	Die Krans	73	Louisvale	39	Vineyards	75
Allesverloren	68	Diemersdal	79	Louwshoek-Voorsorg		Rustenberg	39
Alphen	36	Die Poort	75	Co-operative	60	Rust-en-Vrede	31
Altydgedacht	79	Domein Doornkraal	74	Lutzville Co-operative	70	Saxenburg	32
Ashton Co-operative	62	Drie Berge Plaaskelder	74	Mamreweg Co-operative	68	Simondium Co-operative	47
Aufwaerts Co-operative	56	Drostdy Co-operative	76	McGregor Co-operative	64	Simonsig	32
Avontuur	22	Du Toitskloof Co-operative	59	Meerendal	79	Simonsvlei Co-operative	47
Backsberg	42	Eersterivier Valleise		Merwespont Co-operative	64	Slanghoek Co-operative	61
Badsberg Co-operative	56	Co-operative	26	Merwida Co-operative	60	Soetwyn Boere Co-operative	75
Barrydale Co-operative	72	Eikendal Vineyards	27	Mon Don	64	Spier	33
Bellingham	50	Fairview	43	Mons Ruber	74	Spruitdrift Co-operative	71
Bergkelder	36	Franschhoek Vineyards	54	Montagu Muskadel Boere	75	Stellenbosch Farmers' Winery	40
Bergsig	57	Co-operative		Montpellier	76	Swartland Co-operative	69
Blaauwklippen	23	Glen Carlou	49	Morgenhof	28	Thelema Mountain Vineyards	40
Bloemendal	79	Goudini Co-operative	59	Mouton Excelsior	55	Theuniskraal	76
Bolandse Co-operative	43	Groot Constantia	16	Muratie	29	Trawal Co-operative	71
Bon Courage	63	Groot Eiland Co-operative	59	Nederburg	46	Tulbagh Ko-operatiewe	
Bonnievale Co-operative	63	Hamilton Russell Vineyards	77	Neethlingshof	29	Wynkelder	76
Boplaas	72	Hartenberg	27	Nordale Co-operative	65	Twee Jongegezellen	77
Boschendal	52	Haute Provence	54	Nuy Co-operative	60	Uiterwyk	34
Botha Co-operative	57	Hemel-en-Aarde Winery	78	Onverwacht	78	Van Loveren	67
Bottelary Co-operative	24	Kaapzicht	38	Opstal	60	Vergenoegd	40
Bovlei Co-operative	78	Kango Co-operative	74	Oude Nektar	30	Villiera	48
Brandvlei Co-operative	58	Kanonkop	38	Overgaauw	31	Villiersdorp Co-operative	61
Buitenverwachting	16	Klawer Co-operative	70	Overhex Co-operative	60	Vlottenburg Co-operative	35
Calitzdorp Co-operative	73	Klein Constantia	18	Paarl Rock	47	Vredendal Co-operative	71
Cederberg Cellars	70	Kloofzicht	76	Perdeberg	47	Vredenheim	35
Citrusdal Co-operative	70	KWV	44	Porterville Co-operative	68	Waboomsrivier Co-operative	61
Clairvaux Co-operative	64	Laborie	45	Rhebokskloof	47	Wamakers Vallei Co-operative	79
Clos Cabrière	54	La Bri	54	Riebeeck Wine Farmers	69	Warwick	41
Clos Malverne	24	Ladismith Co-operative	74	Co-operative		Welgemeend	49
De Doorns Co-operative	58	La Motte	55	Rietrivier Wynkelder		Wellington Wynboere	
De Helderberg Co-operative	25	Landskroon	45	Co-operative	75	Co-operative	79
Delaire	25	Langverwacht Co-operative	64	Robertson Co-operative	65	Welmoed Co-operative	35
Delheim	25	La Provence	55	Romansrivier Co-operative	60	Weltevrede	67
De Wet Co-operative	59	Lebensraum	59	Roodezandt Co-operative	65	Windmeul	49
De Wetshof	64	Lemberg	76	Rooiberg Co-operative	66	Winkelshoek	69
De Zoete Inval	49	Lievland	38	Rozendal Farm	39	Zandvliet	67